# BAYLOR
## AT THE CROSSROADS

# BAYLOR
## AT THE CROSSROADS

Memoirs of a Provost

_____

## DONALD D. SCHMELTEKOPF
Baylor University Provost, 1991–2003

CASCADE _Books_ · Eugene, Oregon

BAYLOR AT THE CROSSROADS
Memoirs of Provost

Cascade Books
An Imprint of Wipf and Stock Publishers
199 W. 8th Ave., Suite 3
Eugene, OR 97401

www.wipfandstock.com

ISBN 13: 978-1-4982-3176-3

*Cataloging-in-Publication data:*

Schmeltekopf, Donald D.

Baylor at the crossroads : memoirs of a provost / Donald D. Schmeltekopf.

x + 134 p. ; 23 cm.

ISBN 13: 978-1-4982-3176-3

1. Baylor University—History. 2. Christian universities and colleges—United States. I. Title.

LD357.7 S35 2015

Manufactured in the U.S.A.                                                08/19/2015

# CONTENTS

———————

*Preface: Author's Note* | vii

1 Getting to Baylor | 1
2 Early Initiatives | 11
3 Reflections on the Future of Baylor | 20
4 Baylor Enters the Big XII | 25
5 Sesquicentennial Council of 150 | 29
6 Reynolds Announces His Retirement | 33
7 Search for a New President | 38
8 The Sloan Presidency: First Years | 43
9 A New Day for Scholarship and Graduate Education | 56
10 University and Distinguished Professors | 63
11 Baylor at a Crossroads | 70
12 The Polanyi Affair | 74
13 Abner McCall's Advice: Planning and Faculty Encouragement | 83
14 Baylor 2012 | 92
15 Significant Changes in the Provost's Office | 101
16 Taking Stock and the Next Transition | 107
17 Standards for Tenure | 112
18 A Colloquy on the Baptist and Christian Character of Baylor | 116
19 Exit | 124

*Epilogue One* | 128
*Epilogue Two* | 131

# PREFACE
## Author's Note

This is a book about my years as the chief academic officer—provost and vice president for academic affairs—of Baylor University from 1991 to 2003. Enormous changes took place at Baylor during these years. On the front end was the charter revision, a change that has permanently restructured the legal governance of the university. On the back end was *Baylor 2012*, a grand vision for the university issued by the Board of Regents on September 21, 2001. The pages before you are my attempt to tell the story, as I experienced it and have reflected on it, of those momentous years of Baylor history.

It is important for the reader to have a sense of the religious context for Baylor at this time. Baylor was founded in 1845 as a Baptist university, affiliated with the Baptist General Convention of Texas (BGCT). This relationship was a point of strength until the 1980s, when fundamentalists gained control of the Southern Baptist Convention (SBC). Although Baylor was not affiliated with the SBC, the fundamentalist movement was seen as a threat to the university if fundamentalists gained control of the BGCT, hence gaining institutional control of Baylor through its legal authority to appoint Baylor's trustees. This potential threat was an all-consuming reality for those responsible for the future of Baylor, especially its president at the time, Herbert H. Reynolds. This threat of the fundamentalist movement was not only present for Baylor; it was present for all Baptist colleges and universities throughout the South.

# PREFACE

The metaphor "crossroads" in the title of this book reflects, in part, this conflict in Baptist life. The official date of the charter change at Baylor was also on September 21, but in 1990, eleven years before *Baylor 2012*. Which path would Baylor take now that it was secure from fundamentalist control, having a self-perpetuating governing board? We were aware that most once-religiously affiliated colleges and universities that had made similar changes in their governance structure, from Harvard to Wake Forest, eventually abandoned their religious tradition altogether, and became secular institutions. Could Baylor mark a different course? This was the central question and challenge for Baylor when I became the chief academic officer.

Readers unfamiliar with Baylor at this time also need to know of a second element of the context for this book. Baylor was primarily a teaching institution in 1991, and had been since its founding. Prompted in part by the charter revision, the issue of a change in mission soon came to the forefront. That is, should Baylor move in the direction of a research university, one in which graduate education and disseminated research were explicitly part of its responsibilities? This too would prove to be a crossroads; the university had to decide which path to take. As this consideration unfolded, a third question arose: could we integrate our commitment to an ever-deeper religious identity with a serious commitment to graduate education and research? To put the matter straightforwardly, could Baylor be a Christian research university?

None of these questions was on my mind when I came to Baylor as vice provost in 1990. But within a few years, they became the passion of my work as provost, and now shape the contours of this book. Of course, as provost, I always worked in the shadow of the president, first Herbert Reynolds and then Robert Sloan. So these memoirs are also very much about their work as chief executive officers of Baylor. Nothing I accomplished was possible without their consent and support. Also, as I hope these pages make abundantly clear, there were many colleagues in common cause with me, without whose collaboration, good work, and sense of Christian vocation, nothing would have been accomplished.

Finally, I wrote these memoirs for two reasons. First, I have been encouraged to do so by several people I have been associated with since 1991. Without exception these individuals care deeply about Christian higher education and about Baylor. Second, I think the story contained in this book is an important one to tell. After all, Baylor is, in my view, a unique place, perhaps the only Christian research university out there today. I trust you will enjoy my telling of this story.

Donald D. Schmeltekopf
Provost Emeritus, Baylor University

# 1

# GETTING TO BAYLOR

In late January 1990 I received a phone call from Professor Robert
Packard of Baylor University. At the time I was provost at Mars Hill
College in Mars Hill, North Carolina. Professor Packard identified himself as the chair of the search committee for a "vice presidential level" position at Baylor. He said without an iota of reluctance, "We have nothing
to talk about unless you are a Baptist. Are you a Baptist?" "Yes," I replied,
"and I am also a deacon at Mars Hill Baptist Church." I was proud and
Bob Packard seemed relieved.

I was aware of the position opening at Baylor—my *alma mater*, 1962.
I had seen an advertisement for it in the *Chronicle of Higher Education* back
in October 1989. More importantly, I had been nominated for the position
by Allen Burris, the vice president and academic dean at Meredith College
in Raleigh, North Carolina, and a close professional colleague. In addition,
Jonathan Lindsey, then head of Baylor libraries and a cousin by marriage,
suggested that I should apply for the position. I had written a letter to the
search committee indicating my interest, but I had heard nothing from
Baylor and, frankly, put the whole matter out of my mind. Now, weeks later,
Bob Packard called to ask if I would be willing to come to Baylor as soon
as possible for a visit with the search committee and others at Baylor, and,
more generally, to become familiar with the Baylor of 1990. I said yes! My
wife, Judy, was to accompany me.

The advertisement for the position was highly unusual—a "vice presidential level" position. What did that mean? What I learned during my visit was that the provost at the time, John Belew, was to retire the end of May 1991. President Herbert H. Reynolds was uncertain about whom he might select as Belew's successor, thus he created an interim, year-long position from July 1990 to May 31, 1991. This gave Reynolds virtually a full year to sort things out, with the addition of a new senior level administrator from whom to choose. Furthermore, because Reynolds saw all vice presidential positions as essentially equal, no one in his mind was "number two." As a result, I visited Baylor not really knowing what position I might be a candidate for down the road. Could it be chief academic officer, head of student life, chief administrative officer, or what?

My visit to Baylor was in February of 1990. On the evening of the first day, Judy and I attended a dinner meeting with all the members of the search committee and their spouses. The search committee was a large one, composed of about fifteen members. Most of the committee members were tenured faculty members and several were department chairs. Bob Packard was typical: professor of physics and chair of the department. There were also a few staff members on the committee as well as a student member I never met.

The dinner and discussion were enjoyable. I really could not tell in several cases who was on the search committee and who was the committee member's spouse; that's how open the discussion was. Though the committee wanted to know something about who I was and what I had done, mainly they wanted to talk about Baptist politics and to get my views on the big issues, such as what I thought about the Southern Baptist Convention and its move to a political fundamentalism. They were interested in what was happening among North Carolina Baptists, especially the Baptist State Convention of North Carolina. I was very familiar with these matters. I had been an active player in North Carolina Baptist life, and knew a good deal about Texas Baptist life since two of my brothers, Edward and Robert, were both pastors in Texas. In fact, Edward was at the time associate executive director of the Baptist General Convention of Texas.

After the dinner meeting, Judy and I drove around Waco a bit to unwind. We both had a positive response to the conversation that took place. I thought things might go well, but they seemed to go better than either of us anticipated. Ann Miller, professor of English and wife of committee-member Bob Miller, professor of political science and chair of the department, whispered to me as we were leaving, "You are so articulate!" That comment got my attention. I began to wonder, is it possible we might be coming to Baylor? The thought was both pleasant and a bit overwhelming. Frankly, I wondered if I would be getting into water over my head.

The next day I met with the search committee first thing in the morning. We discussed the academic situation at Baylor as well as other aspects of campus life. The committee also wanted to know my views on higher education, especially as these might relate to Baylor, a large Baptist university. One matter became very clear to me: in some ways, Baylor was not much different than Mars Hill College. Faculty expectations focused on teaching, not research. The standard teaching responsibility was four courses per semester. There was no mention at all about graduate education. The term was never used. Of course, Baylor was a national university, not a regional college. Furthermore, Baylor played big-time sports and competed with other national universities. And Baylor was a comprehensive university, not just an undergraduate institution.

The really important meeting of the second day occurred with Clif Williams, a member of the search committee, a long-time professor of management, and, I learned later, a trusted associate of President Reynolds. The purpose of our meeting, or so it seemed, was for Clif to learn as much about me as he could, particularly the sincerity of my Christian faith. He wanted to know what I truly believed, particularly surrounding the Christian faith. I told him directly at one point early in our conversation, "Clif, I am a believer." He instantly knew what I meant, although I went on to elaborate on my Christian commitments. During that conversation, I also remember asking Clif what, if anything, Baylor might do to stave off a fundamentalist takeover of the university, as had happened with all the Southern Baptist seminaries by 1990. Though he did not know the answer to my question, he was aware that there was "a secret plan." Indeed, there was.

The only other part of our visit was an extensive tour of the campus, led by Ed Davis, an older graduate student in the School of Education. The remarkable and surprising aspect about the search process was that I did not meet with President Reynolds or any other member of the senior administration. My assessment was that Reynolds had confidence in the judgment of the search committee, especially individuals such as Bob Packard, Clif Williams, and Bob Miller. Furthermore, I had no idea what my actual job or status might be were I offered the position (e.g., would I work in the academic division, would I be granted tenure, and, if so, what department would I be affiliated with?) or what the salary would be. Such matters were never discussed and I felt it was premature for me to push on these matters. I did make it clear, however, that I wanted to remain in the academic side of the house; that area best fitted my strengths and experience.

Within two weeks after my return to North Carolina, I received a phone call from President Reynolds offering me the job. He said I would have the title of "vice provost" and that I would work out of the provost's office. He also asked if Judy and I could return to Baylor for another visit in a few weeks in order to give us an opportunity to sort out what I would do, meet the other senior administrators, and look for a house. Further, we agreed on the timing of a public announcement of my appointment in both the Mars Hill and Baylor communities. There was still no mention of salary or tenure status. I was really not concerned about either. I did not have tenure at Mars Hill and I was certain my Baylor salary would surpass what I received at Mars Hill.

## A BACKGROUND EPISODE

In the summer and fall of 1989, a huge effort was made by moderate Southern Baptists to elect Daniel Vestal, then pastor of Dunwoody Baptist Church in Atlanta, to the presidency of the Southern Baptist Convention. One example of this effort was a rally held that fall at the First Baptist Church in Asheville, North Carolina. Influential Baptist leaders, such as Cecil Sherman (a Baylor graduate, pastor of Broadway Baptist Church in Fort Worth, and soon-to-be head of the Cooperative Baptist Fellowship), were the keynote speakers. A Mars Hill colleague of mine, Richard Hoffman, and I attended this rally. We were both moved by what we heard. It was clear that the election of Vestal was probably the last hope of saving the SBC from political fundamentalism and its iron grip on Baptist institutions throughout the south and elsewhere.

During our drive back to Mars Hill that evening, we discussed what we might do to assist the Vestal campaign. We came up with the idea of organizing an effort among the alumni of all Baptist colleges and universities in the south to support Vestal for president of the SBC. The next day we conferred with the president of Mars Hill College, Fred Bentley, and he bought into our plan. We contacted other Baptist leaders in North Carolina, such as Robert Mullinax, executive director of the Council of Colleges and Universities of the Baptist State Convention of North Carolina. He too was enthusiastic about our idea. The big question we faced, however, was who might we recruit to get this drive off the ground? Who had the clout and visibility to get the various Baptist schools and their presidents to cooperate? There was really only one choice: Herbert H. Reynolds, President of Baylor University.

We contacted President Reynolds, told him about our plan, and he agreed to help. He promised to send a personal letter, a draft of which was composed by Mullinax, to all the presidents of the Baptist colleges and universities asking them to meet with him and others at the annual meeting in Atlanta of the Southern Association of Colleges and Schools in December of 1989. The meeting was convened by Reynolds in the late afternoon in a large meeting room of the conference hotel. Many were in attendance, including most of the invited presidents. President Reynolds was masterful in his leadership of the meeting. He pointed out that there are times when presidents of institutions will be called upon to place their jobs on the line. It was clear to everyone that he thought this current conflict in the SBC was one of those times. After some discussion, he focused on strategy. Someone needed to coordinate the effort to work with the alumni of all the schools. Fred Bentley immediately suggested my name, and after getting nods of approval around the room, President Reynolds asked me to do it. Of course, I agreed and thus began an early working relationship with the man who would soon be my president.

A few weeks later I received the telephone call from Bob Packard asking me to come to Baylor to be interviewed. I also learned later that President Reynolds had suggested to Packard that I was someone who should be interviewed, provided I was a Baptist. It never occurred to me when I jumped into the Vestal campaign that it might open a door to Baylor. But apparently it did.

Judy and I returned for a second visit to Baylor and Waco in mid-April. I met with a number of individuals in the senior administration, including a meeting of the President's Cabinet. During the cabinet meeting, Reynolds discussed the program for the upcoming commencement, one element of which was the invocation. It was decided on the spot that the invocation would be given by my brother, Robert, whose daughter was graduating that year. During the visit I also met for the first time with Provost John Belew which gave me an opportunity to get a feel for the academic division and its administrative structure. In addition, while my faculty status was not fully clarified, I agreed with the president that I should be a member of the Department of Philosophy. The other possibility was religion. Given the current climate of Baptist life, it was clearly prudent for me to be in the Department of Philosophy. I was also told what my salary would be, but nothing was said about tenure.

Judy spent her time with a real estate agent looking for a house—with no success. Finally, the evening before we departed, and thanks to Annette and Jonathan Lindsey, we located a house that was being sold by the owners. We settled the next day. Mission accomplished! We moved to Waco on June 29, 1990.

## SERVING AS VICE PROVOST

My year as vice provost was strange, notably out of the ordinary. I had been accustomed at Mars Hill to being in charge, to running things, with many people reporting to me. I now reported to Provost Belew, but nobody reported to me, except a part-time assistant, and, for all intents and purposes, I had no administrative responsibilities. My main job was to attend meetings. These included weekly meetings of the provost's staff, monthly meetings of the Deans' Council, and weekly meetings of the President's Cabinet. There were also a number of other meetings I was required to attend, such as the occasional meetings of the President's Coordinating Council and the bi-monthly meetings of the Board of Regents.

One extraordinary meeting of the Board of Regents (then called the Board of Trustees) was on September 21, 1990. As I have already mentioned above, in my conversation with Clif Williams during the search process, I asked him about the possibility of a hostile takeover of Baylor by those of the fundamentalist movement, rampant in the Southern Baptist Convention at the time. Was Baylor prepared, I wondered, for such an eventuality? I knew that some of the key leaders of the "conservatives" were from Texas, such as Paul Pressler, an appeals court judge from Houston, Paige Patterson, affiliated with the Criswell Center for Biblical Studies in Dallas, and Jimmy Draper, pastor of the First Baptist Church of Euless. Questions were now being asked by such leaders if Baylor needed a course correction, that it had become a "liberal" institution, especially in its religion department which had forsworn a literal interpretation of Scripture, particularly the book of Genesis.

Clif Williams told me he understood that there was a "secret plan" to take on this growing challenge to Baylor's academic independence. On

September 21, as I was sitting in the board room with all the board members and the senior administration of Baylor, including, of course, President Reynolds, the secret plan was revealed before our eyes. The basic move was straightforward: amend the charter of Baylor to make its governing board, now to be called the "Board of Regents," essentially self-perpetuating. The Baylor board would no longer be selected in its entirety by the Baptist General Convention of Texas. Now, only 25 percent would be; the remaining 75 percent would be selected by the regents themselves. There was a spirited debate in the meeting. It was clear that some board members knew in advance what the plan was; others clearly did not. The proposal passed by the required two-thirds majority. I was amazed at what I had witnessed. I had been at Baylor less than three months and suddenly, without any foreknowledge, a change of historic proportion was made. The charter change would increasingly come into play as my work at Baylor unfolded over the next few years.

Though my main job as vice provost was to attend meetings, I did acquire a significant teaching responsibility. Just before our move to Waco, I received a phone call from William Cooper, dean of the College of Arts and Sciences and professor of philosophy, asking if I would be willing to team-teach an introductory philosophy course with him in the upcoming fall semester. Even though I did not know Bill, I readily agreed and we had a successful experience together. This became important not only because I was able to develop a relationship with the dean of the College of Arts and Sciences, but also because Bill's assessment of me would probably be an important factor in my long-term prospects at Baylor.

Perhaps the most significant outcome of my relationship with Dean Cooper was his suggestion to Provost Belew that I have a private visit with each of the academic deans of the university and every department chair of the College of Arts and Sciences. This was done over the course of the 1990-91 academic year. These visits proved extremely beneficial to me in my efforts to get to know Baylor—its people and its culture. I offer two examples. First, my visit with Harold Beaver, chair of the geology department, revealed to me the remarkable spirit of collegiality that existed in that department. It was clear that Dr. Beaver's demeanor had a lot to do with that departmental culture, but it also suggested to me that geologists are team players. As good scientists, they work together not only with one another, but also with students—on field trips and in research projects.

The other example was my visit with Robert Collmer, dean of the Graduate School. Dean Collmer was an accomplished literary scholar, former chair of the English department, and for several years the dean of the Graduate School. I was immediately struck by his realistic appraisal of the graduate program at Baylor. He said forthrightly: "We do graduate education at Baylor on the cheap!" Even though I had little experience with graduate education as an administrator, I knew what he meant. Graduate education at Baylor got minimal financial support and lacked institutional commitment. Now I understood why graduate education never came up at all during my interviews with the search committee.

I don't recall having any private meetings with President Reynolds during the fall semester, although we were together in a lot of contexts. However, in late January 1991, the president came to see me in my office in Pat Neff Hall—unannounced! Somewhat to my surprise at that time, he told me of his decision that I should be the next chief academic officer, succeeding Provost Belew. He also told me that as chief academic officer, I needed to have tenure, and my tenure would be in the philosophy department. Apparently, he had not consulted with the philosophy department about my tenure, or even Dean Cooper. This caused a bit of a dustup in the department. The department members, under the leadership of the chair of the department, Robert Baird, insisted that they be given the opportunity to vote on my tenure. The president acceded to their request, and within a few days, the department agreed unanimously.

During the spring semester 1991, my work as vice provost took on greater focus and seriousness of purpose. One added responsibility was interviewing all prospective faculty members. This had been the practice of chief academic officers at Baylor for years, and was continued by Belew. Provost Belew asked me to join him in all the interviews he would be conducting. One aspect of all candidates' applications was a one-page form that included questions about academic background and past experience, as well as a space to indicate church or denominational affiliation. The interviews typically began with a comment of appreciation by the provost for whatever information was indicated about church/denominational affiliation. He would then ask the candidates if they had any questions about this matter in the Baylor context. Hardly anyone ever did, thus the discussion about Baylor's Christian identity ended.

I reflected on this pattern of faculty interviews, and wondered if we should do more to ascertain the Christian commitments of the faculty members we were hiring. I wasn't sure how to do this at the time, but was convinced we needed to get a deeper sense of the question than was the existing practice. As matters would unfold in the years ahead, the religious component of our faculty interviews became much more substantive, yet also a matter of contention with some members of the Baylor faculty.

My relationship with Baylor colleagues got a considerable boost in late April at a national meeting in Philadelphia on "Internal Development of Leaders." Approximately twenty-five Baylor faculty members and administrators and a student attended at the invitation of President Reynolds. I do not recall the content of specific sessions, but I vividly recall asking all members of the Baylor contingent to meet with me Saturday evening to discuss what we had heard and what initiatives we might undertake at Baylor to develop campus leaders. I was particularly interested in how we might move forward as a Christian university. The response to my ideas was extremely positive, and I sensed a community of support for my upcoming work as chief academic officer.

On May 7, 1991, I had a lengthy meeting with President Reynolds to review some of my observations about Baylor, the academic goals and priorities I had in mind, and some early initiatives I wanted to pursue. I began the discussion with the job description of the "Provost and Vice President for Academic Affairs." (When I was first appointed, my title was simply vice president for academic affairs.) We moved on to discuss some of my concerns and observations. One concern was the intellectual climate of the campus. I saw very little evidence of it. Several sub-cultures were notable, such as Greek life, sports interests, religious emphasis, and fine arts programs, but, I contended, a significant intellectual sub-culture was lacking. I also mentioned that I thought the honors program was languishing, that there were inefficiencies in academic operations (such as low course enrollments in several courses), that the coordination with the various deans was uneven, and that more long-range planning was needed. Then I turned to some specific goals I had in mind, such as a world affairs minor (this was really Reynolds's idea), conversational knowledge of a foreign language, an optional core curriculum and the development of capstone courses, the hiring of minority faculty members, a rethinking of the meaning of scholarship, and the pursuit of the "integration of faith and learning." With respect to the latter, I wanted to establish an initial group of ten faculty members to meet with me regularly to discuss issues surrounding what it means to be a Christian university. I hoped that such a conversation would bring some clarity to this issue, and, importantly, enliven the intellectual culture of the campus.

I also told President Reynolds that I wanted to send a letter to all faculty members asking them for specific suggestions on ways to strengthen the overall university academic program or any part of it. The responses, I said, would not only be informative to me, but would also imply some possible directions for the academic program. In short, I wanted to know what was on the minds of faculty members with respect to academic matters, and I wanted to provide them with an opportunity to tell me. Additionally, I planned to have a deans' retreat in August in order to discuss some of my ideas with the deans across campus, to hear from them about their ideas and concerns, and to build relationships.

President Reynolds seemed to be pleased with our meeting; in fact, he offered suggestions along the way that were helpful to me. When the meeting was done, I believed we were on the same page. Indeed, we were!

# 2

# EARLY INITIATIVES

A few concrete academic goals began to crystallize in my mind by the
time I started my tenure as the chief academic officer of Baylor on
June 1, 1991. The two preeminent ones were the strengthening of the core
curriculum and the integration of faith and learning. I believed that if we
could make real progress on these two fronts, Baylor's long-term identity
as a first-rate Christian university would be much enhanced. Fortunately, I
was able to provide leadership for both these goals.

Baylor had a recent but unsuccessful history attempting to reform its
core curriculum, or general education. The report of the 1984–86 Institutional Self-Study for the Southern Association of Colleges and Schools, directed by Robert Baird, called specifically for the creation of a presidential
task force "to study and make recommendations for revisions in the core
curriculum." Thus, in 1988 President Reynolds appointed a large university-wide committee for the purpose of reviewing and making recommendations concerning Baylor's core curriculum. The chair of the committee
was Professor J. R. LeMaster, respected long-time member of the English
department.

Campus conversations on general education were being held at this
time all across higher education in the United States. President Reynolds
was very much aware of this national discussion, as were Bob Baird and
other leaders of the faculty. In fact, the final report of the self-study team

made significant reference to the work of the American Association of Colleges on this subject, which in its various reports bemoaned the lack of coherence of most core curricula in our nation's colleges and universities and advocated common intellectual experiences. Unfortunately, after months of study and meetings, the university-wide committee appointed by President Reynolds found itself hopelessly in a stalemate. Because the committee could reach no agreement on what should be done to revise the core, the chair, Jim LeMaster, recommended that the committee be dissolved. And so it was!

As I understood the matter from informal conversations with a few faculty members, the underlying reason for the stalemate in the committee was the competing interests of the various academic departments represented, especially within the College of Arts and Sciences. The general education curriculum was essentially a set of disciplinary introductory courses taken by all undergraduates, regardless of major, as was the typical approach across the country. Departmental representatives on the committee understandably recognized that if they were to surrender any course requirements in the general education program, they would likely lose significant revenue, the funds needed to support the respective departments. The resistance to change that resulted in a stalemate was not philosophical, but pragmatic and historical. Long-settled curricular arrangements should not be disturbed.

The proposal I put on the table, and discussed with President Reynolds in our May meeting, was an "optional core curriculum." This plan would leave in place the existing distribution-requirements approach to general education, but add as an alternative or option for a limited number of students a much-enhanced notion of a core curriculum, one that would feature a high degree of structure and coherence. Further, the content of the courses would be centered in the biblical and Christian tradition, the achievements of Western civilization, an understanding of world affairs, and other fields, such as historical consciousness and mathematical reasoning, provided they contributed to coherence overall. This version of our core curriculum, I maintained, should embody a vision of what we believed most nearly approximated the qualities of an educated person.

We now needed a number of respected faculty members who would agree to work as a group to create such an optional core curriculum. I conferred extensively with Dean Cooper for names of about twenty-five faculty members to serve on the committee. The most important person would be the chair of this group; we both agreed it should be Bob Baird. I visited with Baird at length about the proposal. Because he had already been disappointed about the work of the presidential task force on reforming the general education program, an effort he had specifically recommended as project director of the 1984–86 Self-Study, Baird wanted to be sure I was serious about moving forward. I was extremely pleased when Professor Baird agreed to serve as chair. Not only that, he suggested names of others he wished to see on the committee. By the end of the summer of 1991, the committee was named and prepared to get on with its work.

The committee worked over the course of two years to develop a rationale for the new curriculum and the actual courses that would be included. The committee engaged in a great deal of research on core curriculum issues and visited widely with departments of the university to get input on the new curriculum. All the courses proposed were interdisciplinary in nature and virtually all were team-taught. The goal of the new curriculum was to encourage "learning communities" that were formed by active learning and the reading of primary texts. And the name of the new curriculum would be the Baylor Interdisciplinary Core (BIC).

Here is what prospective students read about the "Baylor Interdisciplinary Core" on Baylor's website today, more than two decades later:

> The primary objective was to create an interdisciplinary curriculum, because, after all, life is interdisciplinary. It was decided that courses should be team-taught by professors from across the university and the community to offer a variety of perspectives within one course. As part of the courses, students would participate in active learning, which requires them to play a role in their own education. Students read primary sources instead of commentaries found in textbooks. They read Plato instead of reading about Plato. . . . In addition, studies found that a common experience in which students progress through the courses together enhances their education, so the committee determined that BIC students would progress through the BIC sequences together. In order to develop this common experience, students would enter the BIC at the beginning of their university education.

When the work of the committee was completed, the next hurdle was to get the faculties of the various schools to approve it. This was accomplished by the end of the spring semester of 1993—by an overwhelming majority across the university. Not only was the new core curriculum attractive in its own right, but it also was presented as "optional," meaning that students made the decision themselves whether they would participate. Furthermore, the number of students permitted to enter the program was limited to two hundred per year.

The first class of BIC students was admitted in 1995. In the intervening two years, however, faculty for the various courses were recruited and syllabi developed. Released time for faculty preparation had to be provided. Fortunately, Dean Cooper, who strongly advocated for the program, was able to find most of the faculty development funds in his own college budget. In addition, Baylor received a substantial grant from the National Endowment for the Humanities to support our faculty development efforts for the new core curriculum. Between Dean Cooper's support and the NEH grant, we were able to prepare our participating faculty very well to teach in the new program.

Now in its twentieth year, BIC has been and will continue to be a successful program. It has had enthusiastic faculty participation, strong student enrollment, and a record of alumni achievement. One of my favorite events of the academic year was the annual banquet for the BIC students and faculty held late in the second semester. [Note: The administrative director of BIC reported to me until it became a part of the Honors College in 2002.] The *esprit de corps* at each occasion was palpable. I did not observe such a sense of community among students in any other academic program at Baylor. That spirit, along with the educational quality of the program, sets BIC apart and today distinguishes it as one of the four academic components of the Honors College. In fact, my view is that BIC was an important forerunner for the eventual launching and institutional embracing of our excellent Honors College.

The integration of faith and learning, my second early initiative at this time, was portentous, and would become enormously significant for Baylor during my years as provost and those that followed. I had been thinking about the faith-learning interface since my years at Mars Hill College, where one day in chapel, Robert Melvin, a Baylor graduate and distinguished member of Mars Hill's religion faculty, described the Christian college as a "community of faith and learning." The light went on in my head. Yes, that's it! I had not heard the distinctive identity of a Christian college spoken in that way before, but it immediately and intuitively seemed true.

The most important idea I brought to Baylor was "faith and learning." I soon found a conversation partner in Professor Michael Beaty of the philosophy department. The problem of the faith/learning interface, Mike argued, was primarily intellectual, not one of religious devotion. I knew that this was something we needed to talk about at Baylor, particularly in light of the charter change. Could Baylor be an ever-more serious Baptist and Christian university in light of the fact that we were no longer "controlled" by the Baptist General Convention of Texas? How could we deepen the understanding of our Christian identity as a first-rate academic institution? How could this view come to be widely shared in the Baylor community?

As I had articulated to President Reynolds, my initial strategy was to recruit ten respected faculty members to join with me every three weeks for a breakfast meeting to discuss questions the group would formulate themselves. I also thought this first group should be made up entirely of Baptists and be broadly representative of the faculty as a whole. The first "Faith and Learning Group" consisted of the following faculty members: Bob Baird and Mike Beaty, philosophy; Bill Cooper, Dean of the College of Arts and Sciences; Stephen Gardner, economics; Georgia Green, music; William D. Hillis, vice president for student life; Ann Karaffa, education; David Slover, religion; Elizabeth Vardaman, business; and Clif Williams, management. Our agenda was always the same: We met in the Harrington House beginning with breakfast at 7:15 am, followed by a devotional and a time of sharing mutual concerns. (It was astonishing how many deaths occurred that year within the families represented in the group.) And then we turned to a discussion of the questions we had formulated for ourselves. Each participant submitted five questions, and these then were organized into an overall collection of approximately fifty questions. We focused on these questions for the entire academic year. This procedure was repeated for five years, with ten different faculty members each year. Thus, by the end of the 1995-96 academic year, fifty faculty members had participated with me in these "faith and learning" discussion groups.

Here are twelve questions, formulated by the participants themselves, which serve as typical examples of what we asked ourselves in the discussion groups over the five-year period.

1. What is meant by a "Christian university"? Is it a Christian faculty? Is it a Christian student body? Are the courses taught differently? If the courses are not taught differently, what makes a Christian university distinctive from a non-Christian university? Is there such a thing as "Christian physics" or "Christian English"?

2. What are the distinguishing characteristics of a Christian university that mark it as different from a secular university?

3. What is meant by a Christian worldview? How would a formalized statement of a Christian worldview read for Baylor University?

4. If one accepts that "all truth is God's truth" and that for the Christian there is no sacred or secular, what are the implications for the curriculum and the way that the curriculum is taught?

5. Is there a distinction to be made between the teaching of a Christian biologist and the teaching of "Christian biology"? What, if anything, does this tell us about the teaching of other disciplines in the university?

6. Is there any department (other than perhaps religion) that does a good job of avoiding putting religion and academia into two spheres? If so, what can we learn from those groups or individuals? What is the meaning of integrating faith and learning?

7. What can be done to ensure a solid, Christian faculty will be here in AD 2020?

8. How do we select and mentor faculty in a way that supports the ideals of a Christian university while maintaining diversity in the faculty? Can this be done?

9. A number of contemporary Ivy League schools have their roots in evangelical religious revival. In their pursuit of academic excellence, these institutions left their Christian roots entirely. How does Baylor commit to academic excellence without the same result?

10. Why have Protestants failed, in the twentieth century, to develop institutions that are, as George Marsden said, "Christian in any interesting sense"?

11. A Christian university with a serious graduate school is unusual. What should be the goals of Baylor's graduate school?

12. Is an education at Baylor University different from an education at the University of Texas at Austin? If so, how?

When I started these faith and learning discussion groups in the fall of 1991, I was careful to avoid bringing attention to what we were doing. In fact, I mentioned to President Reynolds in our May 7 meeting that these discussion groups would be about "thinking, not acting." However, after three years, the word got around and some faculty members were concerned. For example, of the questions formulated by the final group in 1995-96, one was: "Why are many of the faculty so anxious about the faith and learning issue? And what could the administration do to calm this anxiety?" One prominent faculty member told me directly: "Don, you need to back off the faith and learning agenda."

The faith-learning discussion on campus was accompanied by a fortuitous development at Valparaiso University: the creation in 1990-91 of the Lilly Fellows Program in Humanities and the Arts and its offspring, the National Network of Church-Related Colleges and Universities. The Lilly Fellows Program (LFP) was funded, as the name suggests, by the Lilly Endowment and provided for post-doctoral studies at Valparaiso for those who wanted to pursue careers in Christian higher education. The National Network was a new collaboration of (initially) twenty-five Christian colleges and universities from across the United States who would meet annually in the fall to discuss the major issues faced by these schools. Baylor, through the office of President Reynolds, was invited to be one of the charter members of the National Network. President Reynolds, in turn, asked Bob Baird and me to be Baylor's two representatives at the annual conference. Other charter members included—in addition to Valparaiso—Boston College, Calvin College, Fordham University, Furman University, Loyola Marymount University, Roanoke College, University of Notre Dame, Pepperdine University, and Wheaton College.

The founding director and overall head of the LFP and the National Network was Mark Schwehn, then professor of humanities and dean of Christ College at Valparaiso. The inaugural meeting of the National Network was in October 1991 at Valparaiso. Baird and I attended, representing Baylor, though our expenses for the conference were covered by the Lilly Endowment. The enormously stimulating conference combined superb lectures by distinguished speakers, discussion of important issues, exciting exchanges with others in attendance, and corporate worship in the enormous chapel at Valparaiso. Having never experienced such a conference before in my professional life, I was proud to be in the presence of others who were both serious Christians and serious scholars/academics.

In the closing session of the conference, Schwehn addressed some plans for the National Network that he hoped to implement, including the creation of a governing board for the network. Those in attendance supported the idea and Schwehn asked me to be a member of the first board, serving a three-year term. Another element of Schwehn's agenda was the sponsorship of regional conferences, hosted by network schools. Baird and

I embraced this idea, took it to our faith-learning discussion group back at Baylor, and proceeded to plan a regional conference of all the church-related colleges and universities in Texas, to be held in April of 1992. We were "acting" after all.

Twenty-six Texas colleges and universities were represented at our first regional conference. The theme was simply "Faith and Learning," sponsored by Baylor and the Lilly Fellows Program, since as a network school, Baylor received five thousand dollars to support the costs of the conference. The keynote speakers were Nicholas Wolterstorff, Professor of Philosophical Theology at Yale, and Mark Schwehn. The conference was a tremendous success not only for those in attendance from other schools, but primarily for those of us at Baylor. The Baylor participants seemed to be increasingly intrigued by the notion of integrating faith and learning.

We continued to sponsor LFP regional conferences for several years, usually held on our campus, and these conferences, together with the National Network and our active participation in it, gave us professional colleagues in Christian higher education nationwide that most of us at Baylor had not known before. At least in my own case, the overwhelming majority of Christian scholars I knew up to this point were from within the Baptist context. Now we were in significant conversation with a wide range of scholars and leaders in Christian higher education: Catholic, Lutheran, Reformed, Methodist, Churches of Christ, and several evangelical denominations. This ecumenical yet broadly orthodox community came over time to define increasingly Baylor's religious identity. Until the 1990s, Baylor's mark of religious distinction was that we were "the largest Baptist university in the world." By the year 2000, that language disappeared almost entirely from the stock of terms used to describe ourselves, whether at the board level, the administrative level, or at the faculty level.

Not everyone in the Baylor community was happy with this turn of events. As I noted above, the faith-learning agenda disturbed some of our constituency, especially some faculty members. Given the charter change, one assumption seemed to be that religious talk within the university would recede into the background. On the other hand, President Reynolds had assured the critics of the charter change that Baylor was now free to be more faithfully Christian and Baptist than ever before, on its own terms. After the charter change, he gave speeches to that effect across much of Texas. In addition, he appointed an ad hoc university-wide committee in 1990 on the Baptist and Christian character of Baylor. Although, to my knowledge, nothing came of the work of this committee, it nevertheless signaled Reynolds's determination that Baylor stay on course with our Baptist and Christian identity.

# 3

# REFLECTIONS ON
# THE FUTURE OF BAYLOR

---

In early June of 1992, President Reynolds informed four of Baylor's five vice presidents that he would like for each of us to address the Board of Regents at its July meeting on our respective visions for Baylor. The four were Bill Hillis, vice president for student life; Jim Netherton, vice president for administrative affairs; Mike Bishop, vice president for public relations; and me. We would have twenty to twenty-five minutes each for our remarks, and then we would entertain questions or comments from members of the board.

It was a daunting assignment for me. I had been at Baylor only two years and now was being asked to cast a vision for the university. I hardly knew where to begin. Fortunately, toward the end of June 1992, I received an important document from Nathan Hatch, then vice president for graduate studies and research at Notre Dame, whom I had met at a large Baptist meeting on "Integrating Personal Faith and Professional Discipline" at Samford University on June 22–24, 1992. Hatch was one of the featured speakers at the meeting, along with George Marsden, who was then professor of history at Duke University. I hosted a reception in my suite on Friday evening, June 23, for all Baylor participants—about thirty in number—and several of the featured speakers. I was particularly interested in getting to know Hatch and Marsden.

The document Hatch sent me was entitled "Colloquy of the Year 2000," a forty-page statement of Notre Dame's aspirations as a Catholic university for the 1990s. The work on this statement was prompted by the advent of the presidency of Father Monk Malloy, who had succeeded legendary Notre Dame president, Father Theodore Hesburg. As I read the statement, I was struck by how applicable most of its aspirations were for Baylor, and a vision for Baylor began to materialize in my mind. But there was a potential problem: Notre Dame was Catholic. To be able to cast a vision for Baylor, I really needed a Protestant model, not a Catholic one. But no Protestant model existed. Harvard, Yale, Princeton, and Brown had abandoned their Christian foundations well over a century ago. In the twentieth century, all the great Methodist universities had essentially done the same thing: Duke, Vanderbilt, Emory, Northwestern, Southern California, Drew, and even Southern Methodist.

As a result, for the purpose of my "reflections on the future of Baylor," as I stated at the Board of Regents' meeting on July 16, 1992, Notre Dame was the model. I noted first, however, that the charter change was *the* pivotal event for Baylor at that time. I said, "If we could fast forward to the year 2025, we would say that Baylor was at a critical crossroads in the early 1990s regarding its future as a serious Christian university." To face this crossroad, we needed a framework for our vision, and I argued that we should draw on the Roman Catholic higher education community for that framework, specifically Notre Dame.

I emphasized that the Christian commitments of Baylor, together with our "unique standing in the evangelical-Christian higher education community," gave us an opportunity "to achieve nothing short of greatness." Then I moved to the analogy of Notre Dame, saying:

> Over the past two decades or so, the University of Notre Dame has been committed to the mission to be at once "intellectual and Catholic: to pursue learning of the highest quality and to raise issues pertinent to the broadest understanding of Catholic intellectual traditions. The goal is to educate students in a setting where the Catholic faith is alive and taught" (from a pamphlet entitled "Notre Dame's Quiet Revolution").

I noted that while not long ago Notre Dame was known nationally primarily for its football team, by 1992 it already ranked in the top twenty for the quality of its undergraduate student body and in the top sixteen for the size of its endowment. Further, I stated that it had a faculty of growing national reputation and a new level of quality of graduate education. Then I spoke these words: "I am convinced that Baylor can be to Baptists and to the wider evangelical-Christian community what Notre Dame is becoming for the Roman Catholic community, both in America and internationally."

Next, I reflected briefly on the distinctiveness of a Christian university. It is not "mushy value talk" that makes it truly distinctive, nor a "Christian environment," as important as that is. Rather, "it is the real and expressed belief that the university community . . . sees its work and its understanding of the world in relation to God." Then I quoted these words from Richard G. Hutcheson Jr., writing in the *Christian Century* (September 28, 1988): "At [the heart of Christian higher education is] the Christian proclamation that there is a sovereign God, incarnate in Jesus Christ and attested by the biblical revelation, and that this reality shapes the meaning and purpose of human existence." The basis of our distinctiveness at Baylor, I maintained, is that, with Martin Luther, we take our stand: "We acknowledge and seek openly to advance the Christian worldview, that there is a sovereign God, incarnate in Christ, who gives purpose to our lives."

I acknowledged openly that this way of seeing Baylor would meet with "formidable obstacles." First, there would be a defensiveness on the part of many faculty members about linking their professional work with the Christian tradition, the evangelical tradition. After all, Baylor is not a church. Why is this theological outlook even relevant? If one is an economist or psychologist, one gains credibility and status by publishing in his or her own field, the standards for which are established by a professional guild. Furthermore, the ascendancy of fundamentalism in the Southern Baptist Convention raised the specter that embracing such evangelical perspectives could get us too close to the very forces that drove our charter change in the first place.

The second obstacle was uncertainty regarding the level of support in the wider Baylor community for a university that is serious about integrating faith and learning. Many if not most would prefer that the two be separate, letting the Baptist Student Union handle the faith part and the faculty handle the learning part. The two should go their separate ways.

Faced with such obstacles, and others, how might we proceed? I asked. How can we at Baylor become a great university, one that is both excellent and Christian? I proceeded to offer three suggestions, one relating to process and two relating to content. With respect to process, I suggested that in light of the obstacles we faced, we needed a catalyst to give credibility to our future as a great Christian university. This catalyst could take the form of a major strategic planning effort, one that would engage not only the Baylor community but also Baptists and other Christians from across the United States. In effect, I proposed that we "create a national blue-ribbon commission on the future of Baylor University." This strategic planning effort would help build a consensus for our direction as a Baptist and Christian university, and bring a new-found visibility to Baylor in the higher education community. (As it turned out, a year later President Reynolds established the Sesquicentennial Council of 150, a national group of educators, clergy, other professionals, and business leaders designed to accomplish the sort of goals I suggested in this speech to the Board of Regents. More on the work of this body will be discussed below.)

My second suggestion, which came right out of the "Colloquy of the Year 2000," was to increase substantially the number of endowed chairs at Baylor. I stated: "In order to be an effective and respected Baptist university, we need an infusion of talented senior academic people who genuinely want to be a part of a learning community in which the Christian faith is alive." At the time, Baylor had a number of endowed positions, but by and large these positions were only partially funded. The number of fully endowed chairs was exceedingly small, thus giving us very little leverage in recruiting top scholars, such as "the C. S. Lewises and Elton Truebloods of our time."

My third suggestion built on the second and called for what George Marsden, in his address at Samford University in June 1992, referred to as "Christian graduate studies." The general idea of Christian graduate studies, as I presumed Marsden meant it, is that Christian beliefs and intellectual traditions be what graduate students confront in their graduate experiences. This engagement might be integrated into the student's curriculum and actively pursued in colloquia, discussion groups, faculty-student seminars, and the like. On the part of faculty, I suggested that while advancing their work in the secularized professional context, faculty raise for themselves and their students questions that Christian thought and belief might illuminate. Christian scholarly work should be broadly encouraged on the part of Baylor's faculty.

When I finished my remarks, there was a period of questions and comments from the members of the Board of Regents. It was a friendly give-and-take, although I do not recall any specific points made. However, I remember very well what President Reynolds whispered to me when I took my seat next to him: "Superb," he said. (He had no idea what I was going to talk about.) When we left the meeting room for lunch, I asked influential board member, John Baugh of Houston, what he thought of my talk. "I reveled in it," he responded. Those two comments were all I needed to feel confident about what I had said. Notre Dame was our model and the faith/learning agenda was on target.

# 4

# BAYLOR ENTERS THE BIG XII

A remarkable turn of events occurred for Baylor in late 1993 and early 1994: the creation of the Big XII athletic conference. The creation of this new conference represented a merger of the existing universities in the Big Eight Conference—Iowa State, Kansas State, Oklahoma State, Colorado-Boulder, Kansas, Missouri-Columbia, Nebraska-Lincoln, and Oklahoma—and four universities from the old Southwest Conference—Baylor, Texas-Austin, Texas A&M, and Texas Tech. Baylor's inclusion in this new athletic conference was a big deal. After all, schools such as Rice, SMU, and TCU were left out. Baylor was the only private school to be invited to join the Big XII at its inception, and the Board of Regents of Baylor formally voted to join the Big XII in a called meeting on February 23, 1994.

A surprising element of membership in the Big XII, at least for many of us at Baylor, was that the new conference turned out to be about far more than just athletics. We suddenly had a new and expanded set of peer institutions, all of which were major research universities, except Baylor. In the old Southwest Conference, the matter of being a research university wasn't an issue, but in the Big XII, it was; Baylor was the outlier. We could be in the same league in athletics, but we were not in the same league with respect to research and funding for research, or in the area of doctoral-level graduate work. We remained primarily an undergraduate teaching institution, albeit with a reputable law school, that was home to a competitive football team.

Our status as a comprehensive university, or at the time "Doctoral II," as designated in the Carnegie Classification of Colleges and Universities, came glaringly into focus by 1996 when we began play in the new Big XII. Within a year, various top administrators of the new conference schools met regularly to get to know each other and share common concerns. One of those regular meetings was of the provosts which had been a tradition among the schools of the Big Eight but were not of the Southwest Conference. In fact, I did not know a single provost of any of the Southwest Conference schools before 1996. The Southwest Conference had become strictly an athletic conference, and as far as I knew, no one—perhaps other than the school presidents—considered it otherwise.

One of the earliest impressions I got at these profitable meetings—the first in the fall of 1997 held in Kansas City and organized by James Coffman, the provost at Kansas State—was the significant ways the other schools differed from Baylor. The intense conversations that took place about the amount of state funding available for the respective schools and the state politicians who needed to be lobbied in the schools' behalf, for example, emphasized the fact that the eleven other schools were all state universities. It was not the sort of conversation one would hear at Baylor, except insofar as it dealt with the Tuition Equalization Grant program, supporting eligible students from Texas with tuition funds to attend a private university in Texas. Needless to say, I felt a bit out of place.

In one of the early Big XII provosts meetings, we had an open and frank discussion about the amount of discretionary funds available to each of us. A few of the provosts stated that they had five million dollars. Others had around one million and some had in the range of five hundred thousand to seventy-five hundred thousand dollars. Since I was the provost who raised this question, I was in position to answer last. There was just one provost other than me who had not spoken to the question, the provost at the University of Texas-Austin. He said one hundred thousand dollars. I immediately chimed in to report that one hundred thousand dollars was about what I had at Baylor, though this was a bit of an exaggeration. When I became the chief academic officer in 1991, the amount was sixty thousand dollars. My discretionary budget received 5 percent increases each year, more or less, but this would still not have reached one hundred thousand dollars by 1998. Frankly, I was embarrassed about the weak hand I had at Baylor in comparison to almost everyone else. Besides, I was sure that the provost at Texas could easily get to money if he needed it. I reported this exchange to then President Robert Sloan, and it had the desired effect over the coming years. In fact, by the time I left the provost's office in 2003, I had a five hundred thousand dollar discretionary fund under my control. This was a step in the right direction.

In 2001, I hosted two Big XII provosts meetings. The first meeting was actually held in a Dallas resort hotel in February. Other administrators, such as deans and directors, met at the same time in the same hotel. We all ate together in a common dining area, but we had our own separate meetings. Though the event was not in Waco, my role as "host" was to arrange for accommodations, food, meeting rooms, and cost.

The second meeting was held on the Baylor campus in November. One of the purposes of these meetings was for all of us to get to know the various Big XII campuses. Professor Robert Reid, then retired as a long-time Baylor faculty member and chair of the history department, regaled the group with wonderful Baylor stories during a tour of the campus on the afternoon of the first day. That evening we all gathered at the home of a faculty member for hors d'oeuvres and "beverages" before we reassembled on campus for dinner. I led a prayer of thanksgiving for the food, explaining beforehand that this practice was standard at Baylor. They all understood and, in fact, seemed appreciative.

The agenda for the meeting was varied and interesting. After our dinner, Big XII commissioner, Kevin Weiberg, delivered a presentation on "Academic Standards and Big 12 Athletic Programs." Plenary sessions the next day included the following topics: "Core Curriculum and Honors Programs," arranged by Nancy Mergler, provost at Oklahoma; the Baylor Interdisciplinary Core, led by David Hendon, professor of history at Baylor, and Bob Baird; and "New Approaches to Regional Accreditation," led by Ronald Douglas, provost at Texas A&M, and Jon Pitts, special assistant to the provost. As all of these sessions attest, the gatherings of the Big XII provosts were both enjoyable and substantive. Along the way, friendships were created that made our common enterprise even more meaningful, at least to me.

Baylor's participation in the Big XII played a significant role in our elevated academic aspirations. Indeed, in 2006, twelve years after the Board of Regents voted to join the Big XII, Baylor was classified as a research university—"high research activity"—in the Carnegie Classification of Colleges and Universities, as defined by the number of research doctoral degrees awarded annually and by the amount of grant and research dollars received annually. Research and doctoral-level graduate work had become part of Baylor's identity. We were no longer an outlier in the Big XII.

I will conclude this chapter with some interesting footnotes on the careers of some of my fellow provosts in the Big XII. Mark Yudof of Texas eventually became the president of the University of California system, retiring as president in 2013, and succeeded by Janet Napolitano. Brady Deaton from Missouri-Columbia later became the president of that campus, retiring also in 2013. Wallace Loh from Colorado-Boulder became the president of the University of Maryland-College Park in 2010. David Shulenberger from Kansas became the vice president for the Association of Public and Land-grant Universities, retiring in 2010. And Phil DiStefano, who followed Loh as provost at Colorado-Boulder, later became the chancellor of that campus and remains in that position. One of the reasons I mention these particular individuals is because I have been able to follow their careers over the past decade by keeping up with their accomplishments—and, in some cases, controversies—through the national media.

# 5

# SESQUICENTENNIAL
# COUNCIL OF 150

---

In chapter 3, "Reflections on the Future of Baylor," I noted the importance of a strategic planning effort to give "credibility to our future as
a great Christian university." During the speech I made before the Board
of Regents on July 16, 1992, I called for "a national blue-ribbon commission on the future of Baylor University." I knew at the time that President
Reynolds liked my talk—he told me so—but I had no idea his mind had
been moving in the same direction.

By the spring of 1993, President Reynolds had organized a "Sesquicentennial Council" of 150 people to do basically what I had called for
in my speech. The establishment of this council was to coincide with the
150th anniversary of Baylor's founding in 1845. The interim report of the
council stated the purpose and range of its work:

> The Sesquicentennial Council of 150 is a select group of leaders
> in the fields of business, education, entertainment, law, govern-
> ment, medicine, ministry, music, and various other professions
> from 76 cities across America and from the Atlantic and Pacific
> hemispheres. The Council was charged with the responsibility of
> examining and evaluating all aspects of the Baylor community
> to develop specific suggestions for the improvement of current

operations in the 1990s and to make recommendations designed to enhance the work of the University in the 21st century. Several sessions involving all the members of the Council, as well as numerous smaller task force meetings, were held in May, August, and November 1993 (*Leadership & Vision for the 21st Century*).

An executive summary of the Sesquicentennial Council's work was presented by President Reynolds to the entire council and other members of the Baylor community in a celebratory convocation on November 13, 1993. The final report was submitted to the Board of Regents on July 21, 1994.

One of the most noteworthy recommendations from the council was the very first under the heading of "Mission, Governance, and Organization": "*The Primary Goal of Baylor University* is to be one of the foremost universities in the world, expanding its heritage around the globe with graduates committed to leadership and service as world citizens." In other contexts, President Reynolds's language was that Baylor should be "the foremost Christian university in the world." With or without the Christian distinction, it was an ambitious statement for an institution that had focused largely on undergraduate education in the previous 150 years of its existence.

Some members of the council expressed a vision probably borrowed from the business community, "world class." As Larry Lyon, now dean of Baylor's graduate school, suggested in "Baylor in the 1990s" (*The Baylor Project*), successful business leaders often employed a common language to express their response to global competition— "provide 'world-class' products." Translated in the council's report, Baylor should, as Lyon put it, "build 'world-class' facilities, hire 'world-class' faculty, and become a 'world-class' university." The term "world class" was used in many conversations related to the work of the council. This reflected, it seemed to me, a new-found ambition for Baylor that played back to the charter change. This ambition would eventually come to the forefront again in *Baylor 2012*, the ten-year vision document issued in 2001. I will say more about this later.

The make-up of the Sesquicentennial Council was remarkable, a tribute largely to the reputations of President Reynolds and the chairman of the council, Drayton McLane, owner of the Houston Astros baseball team. Some of the notable educators included Ernest Boyer, president of the Carnegie Foundation for Advancement of Teaching; Olin C. Robison, president emeritus of Middlebury College; Brad Carson, Baylor alumnus, Rhodes Scholar, and School of Law, University of Oklahoma; Linda Bunnell

Jones, chancellor of the University of Colorado at Colorado Springs; James Scales, president emeritus of Wake Forest University; Mark Schwehn, dean of Christ College at Valparaiso University; Max Sherman, dean of the LBJ School of Public Affairs, University of Texas-Austin; Milburn Price Jr., dean of the School of Music at Samford University; John Silber, president of Boston University; Barrett Hazeltine, professor of engineering at Brown University; Nathan Hatch, vice president for graduate studies and research at the University of Notre Dame; Martin Marty, professor of church history from the University of Chicago; and Daniel W. Tse, president of Hong Kong Baptist University.

Some of the other high-profile names included Judge Abner McCall, president emeritus of Baylor; Daniel Vestal, pastor of Tallowood Baptist Church, Houston; Thomas Phillips, chief justice of the Supreme Court of Texas; Bob Bullock, lieutenant governor of Texas; Kenneth Carlile, vice chairman of the Carlile Companies; Virginia Ball, principal partner of Ball Associates; Cecil Sherman, coordinator of the Cooperative Baptist Fellowship; David Sibley, state senator of Texas; Dellanna O'Brien, executive director of the Women's Missionary Union; Michael Johnson, professional athlete; Virginia Furrow, physician; Richard Maples, president of the Baptist General Convention of Texas; Lyndon Olson Jr., president of Primerica Insurance Holdings and U.S. Diplomat; Henry Holcomb, writer for the *Philadelphia Inquirer*; Jack Loftis, editor of the *Houston Chronicle*; Mike Singletary, linebacker for the Chicago Bears; and Tom Landry, former coach of the Dallas Cowboys.

People of this level of accomplishment are not reluctant to use the language of "world class" and embrace ambitious goals. Perhaps the best example of this appears in the section of the report dealing with graduate education. The Task Force on Graduate and Professional Education Programs recommended that graduate program enrollment be set at 1,500–2,000 students, and that the enrollment be "distributed in at least 40 doctoral programs." At the time, enrollment was approximately 1,200 students, and the graduate school was home to just fourteen doctoral programs. These increases, both in graduate enrollment and doctoral programs, represented an enormous funding challenge for Baylor, one that few of us really understood at the time. Also, these goals were to be accomplished without any leveling off of our commitment to undergraduate education. Indeed, according to the report, the undergraduate experience at Baylor should not only be improved, but also strengthened in some areas and enlarged in others. These were indeed ambitious goals

In re-reading the council's final report as I composed this chapter, I have found it noteworthy how little Baylor's identity as a serious Christian university is considered. Despite specific references to Baylor's "Christian commitment," to our serving "the principles of Christian higher education," and to "spiritual values," these references are within a framework of upholding a Christian ethos, not a model of faith/learning integration. The "institutional environment" is the main context for discussing Baylor's Christian identity. The report states: "Much can be done to create an academic environment in which one is free to discuss matters of faith and practice and in which students feel challenged to discipleship worthy of that heritage." The impression I got as I revisited the report, and had at the time of its writing, was that the issue of faith/learning integration was not on the table for discussion. In fact, the term never appears. It was not yet part of our institutional vocabulary.

That would soon change, however, as Baylor moved toward a successor to Herbert Reynolds as president. The issues surrounding this transition are the subject of the next two chapters.

# 6

# REYNOLDS ANNOUNCES
# HIS RETIREMENT

---

Although it was fairly well-known around Baylor that President Reynolds planned to retire as president and become chancellor in June of 1995, the transition was not announced officially until the homecoming meeting of the Board of Regents in November of 1993. By spring 1994, a search committee of the board had been named, and by the summer of 1994, members of the committee began interviewing prospective candidates—off campus.

I was asked to be interviewed in July, but I had been accepted into the prestigious Institute for Educational Management (IEM) program at Harvard, which ran from July 10 until the end of the month. Quite honestly, I was a little proud of the fact that I could turn down the request for an interview because I would be at Harvard. In response to my schedule conflict, the search committee requested that I meet with them in August in a Dallas hotel.

The Harvard IEM program was an ideal opportunity for me to bone up on current issues surrounding higher education in America, from curriculum matters, to financial management, to institutional leadership. The institute's principal approach to almost every question was the case-study method, leading the participants through case studies all grounded in a specific institutional context. For example, regarding curriculum, one of the major cases was "Designing a New Curriculum at Brooklyn College." This case focused on the development of a new general education program, one with which I happened to be familiar from my days working at the National Endowment for the Humanities. Brooklyn College had received an NEH grant in the mid-1980s to support its new program. A case about financial management arose out of the University of Missouri-Columbia's effort to cut two of their fourteen schools and colleges and reduce the size of seven others.

The case-study leaders and the speakers for the institute were among the nation's finest, including Arthur Levine, then professor in Harvard's Graduate School of Education, director of the institute itself, and newly elected president of Teacher's College of Columbia University; Henry Rosovsky, long-time dean of Harvard College; Kent John Chabotar, vice president for finance and administration at Bowdoin College in Brunswick, Maine; William R. Harvey, president of Hampton University in Hampton, Virginia; and among many others, Sharon Daloz Parks, senior research fellow in leadership and ethics at Harvard Business School and the Kennedy School of Government.

In addition to exposing me to the larger issues surrounding higher education on a broader scale, the institute also gave me the opportunity to reflect in specific ways on the future of Baylor. For example, all program participants were asked to write the four or five things they will do when they return to their respective campuses. Here are the four I wrote:

1. Work to move Baylor to acknowledge its responsibility for enhancing diversity in the student body, in the faculty, and in the administration;

2. Continue to strengthen graduate education;

3. Enhance the infrastructure for the research activity of faculty members; and

4. Continue to press on the Christian identity of Baylor's mission.

The first item on diversity was much influenced by the institute itself and the participants. In fact, during the closing session, I told the entire group—about ninety-five in number from across the United States and Australia—that I had never before been so impressed with the mix of ethnic and racial diversity of a body of people and noted the positive impact that diversity had on me. The last item regarding mission was a frequent topic of conversation during the institute proceedings. And, of course, Baylor's Christian mission was always on my mind.

The other assignment we were given was to write out a one-page dream for the future of the institution we served. Here is "My Dream for Baylor University":

> My dream for Baylor University is that it will become a university whose distinction and excellence reside in its uniting of learning and faith. This means primarily that the intellectual life of Baylor should be shaped and directed by highly talented and capable teacher/scholars and that a large proportion of these teacher/scholars should be genuinely interested in and conversant with the Protestant Christian tradition. The Baylor of my hopes and dreams is a community of learning in which the free and responsible pursuit of truth—in all of its manifestations and with its accompanying uncertainty—is the guiding vision, whether of students or faculty members. In the enactment of this vision, it is my hope that not only will our students come to possess the rich resources of mind and spirit for their lives and communities, to help form a good and meaningful life, but also that our faculty will provide critical insight within their disciplines and intellectual leadership in the larger society, particularly for the Christian community.
>
> Secondarily, my dream means that the total institutional life of Baylor, as a community of learning, is committed to the enrichment of students as human beings, in particular to their spiritual, moral, and personal dimensions, along with their intellectual growth.

Given the secular nature of the Harvard institute, this was not the kind of dream that I was prepared to bring before the other participants. However, the institute did prepare me well, along with the four items on my to-do list above, for my interview in Dallas with the search committee on August 9, 1994, which had been on my mind throughout July in Cambridge, Massachusetts.

My interview with the five or six representatives of the search committee went very well. Although I do not recall specific topics of the conversation, I remember vividly that the conversation was friendly and positive. At least some of the members seemed to be clearly in my corner, that they wanted me to have a successful interview. Emily Tinsley, a well-known Baylor alumna from my era, was one such person. Because she had been the chair of the academic affairs committee of the Board of Regents, we worked together many times over the past several years. At that time, the board met six times per year.

As the search process unfolded over the next few months, I was named one of three finalists for the Baylor presidency. The other two were Thomas Corts, president of Samford University in Birmingham, Alabama, and Paul Powell, president of the Annuity Board of the Southern Baptist Convention. Each of us was interviewed by the full search committee on October 9, 1994, in the DFW Hilton Hotel. The board had hired a distinguished consultant, John Chandler, former president of Williams College, to assist in the search process. I knew Chandler personally from my years at Mars Hill College. In fact, Chandler grew up in the town of Mars Hill and later attended the college, before he transferred to Wake Forest University. He was the first outside speaker I invited to the college after I became the vice president and dean of Mars Hill in 1985.

I was the last of the three to be interviewed. I recall greeting Paul Powell as he left the hotel, which meant that Thomas Corts must have been interviewed first. My session with the committee included a light meal, and then we got down to business. I proposed some serious ideas about Baylor's future and I thought the response and discussion were good. It became evident to me during the course of our meeting, however, that the level of interest in my candidacy was not uniformly high, as though the committee had already decided whom they were going to recommend to the full board. There were two other giveaways: One was a private query, designed, I am sure, to help me in the interview, from a member during a break: "Don, is there any question you would like for me to ask when we resume our meeting?" The other giveaway was that our consultant fell asleep during a portion of the interview.

Two weeks later, at the regular Board of Regents' meeting on October 27–28, 1994, the search committee made its recommendation to the full board: Thomas Corts, the distinguished president of Samford University. To my surprise, and to the surprise of many others, the recommendation was not well received. From what I was able to determine from second-hand sources, a few activists on the board, upon learning of the impending Corts nomination, had begun their own private inquiries regarding who Corts was, what he had done at Samford, and what kind of leadership he would provide for Baylor. Corts was asked to appear at the meeting, presumably to be regaled as the next president of Baylor. But that was not to be the case. Instead, Corts was questioned about several matters, such as the guest speakers he had invited to the Samford campus, a few of whom seemed to be in the fundamentalist camp. This revelation outraged some of the board members, and along with other issues, led to a stalemate on the board about the Corts nomination. As a result, the search process came to an end, and Tom Corts returned quietly to Birmingham, an embarrassed man, but remained president of Samford.

A few days later, I received a phone call from Gale Galloway, the chair of Baylor's Board of Regents and very successful businessman, asking if we could have lunch together on November 23 at the Waco Hilton Hotel. He said frankly, "I want to get to know you better." We had the lunch, had an enjoyable time together, but he did most of the talking.

# 7

# SEARCH FOR
# A NEW PRESIDENT

---

The Board of Regents soon determined that it would act as a committee of the whole to select the new president. The search committee approach had not worked largely because, in my view, there were a number of members of the board who, given their very strong opinions about what kind of individual they wanted as president, did not want to cede any power to a search committee. So the board moved forward with Gale Galloway in charge. It appeared, however, that a lot of maneuvering was going on behind the scenes, as was to be expected.

In December of 1994, Baylor was a contender in the Alamo Bowl in San Antonio. The afternoon before the big evening game, several hundred people gathered to attend a public meeting at the Marriott River Center Hotel, called specifically to discuss the presidential search and what the Baylor board should be looking for in a new president. The agenda included a report on the search process to date, as well as an open discussion designed to give people the opportunity to express their views on the Baylor presidency. Many did.

One who did was Robert Sloan, inaugural dean of Baylor's Truett Theological Seminary, professor of religion in Baylor's religion department, and well-known Baptist preacher. He spoke at the request of Ella Pritchard, an outspoken member of the Board of Regents. Pritchard's request came from the floor, where I happened to be standing near her, and appeared spontaneous to me. Invited to the podium, Sloan—without notes—delivered a coherent statement on the qualities the next Baylor president should have. One of his emphases was upholding the Baptist and Christian character of Baylor. His remarks were warmly received.

In early January of 1995, the board announced five candidates for the presidency, all of whom were to be interviewed by the full board and an advisory committee made up of approximately fifteen people and chaired by Lyndon Olson Jr., a distinguished Baylor graduate and prominent member of the Waco community. Prior to the interviews, which were scheduled to be on campus February 2–3, 1995, one candidate withdrew his name from consideration, and so the four to be interviewed were William Hillis, vice president for student life at Baylor; Max Lennon, former president of Clemson University; Robert Sloan; and me. Each of the candidates was asked to prepare a statement on Baylor University.

My statement was comprised of five brief parts: 1) Baylor: The Current Situation; 2) A Vision for Baylor: The Integration of Our Christian Faith and Academic Mission; 3) Challenges for Baylor; 4) Personal Assets; and 5) Liabilities and Compensations. With regard to first, the "current situation," I pointed to Baylor as the flagship Baptist university in the country, with outstanding students, faculty, and academic programs. I also noted the large body of loyal alumni, first-rate physical facilities, and the new Big XII Conference. All of these positive features positioned Baylor well to meet the challenges ahead, I claimed.

The vision I articulated was one that came right out of Baylor's historic mission as a premier Christian university and my own reflections about that mission since my arrival at Baylor in 1990.

> Baylor's excellence has come from its commitment to unite faith and learning as the highest and best standard by which to measure the life of an individual or of an institution. This mission was reaffirmed by the Board of Regents with their approval of the new mission statement, approved in 1994, the content of which represented a much deeper understanding of the faith/learning agenda at Baylor.
>
> Within the scope of this mission, my vision for Baylor University is, first, to provide an academic program and a nurturing environment that allow undergraduate students to become educated for a thoughtful life that includes service, vocation, citizenship,

global awareness, technological sophistication, moral understanding, obedience to Christ, and reverence for God. Second, I
believe Baylor and its academic community have the obligation to
become an intellectual center and to engage the world as Christian
scholars in our search for truth. This involves the enhancement
of research efforts, particularly in selective graduate programs,
financially supported with new funds. Third, as Baylor embarks
on a new association with members of the Big XII, we must meet
the challenges and exploit the possibilities to become widely recognized as one of the top fifty institutions in the country, not only
in academic and athletic achievement, but also in the quality of
our students' experience.

These words certainly do echo Baylor's 1994 mission statement: "The vision
of the founders and the ongoing commitment of generations of students
and scholars are reflected in the motto inscribed on the Baylor seal: *Pro Ecclesia, Pro Texana.*" This vision affirms the value of intellectually informed
faith and religiously informed education.

Next, I pointed to the significant work ahead: develop a strategic plan
for the university as a whole; enhance our core curriculum, expand international education, and improve technological capabilities; increase student
financial aid; increase the number of endowed chairs and professorships;
augment the influence and ministry of Truett Seminary within Baptist life;
maintain a full commitment to integrity and excellence in intercollegiate
athletics while becoming competitive at the highest level to gain recognition for the university; and sustain and deepen our commitment to the
Christian and Baptist character of Baylor.

The final two parts of my statement spoke to personal assets and personal liabilities as a university president. On the assets side, I emphasized
my years of administrative experience in higher education, particularly
in Christian higher education, and my professional ties with a wide range
of individuals among the various Baylor constituencies in Texas and the
nation. As to liabilities, while very familiar with funding possibilities, I
pointed to the fact that I had not worked extensively with donors in personal solicitation.

My interview with the full board occurred on Thursday evening, February 2, and my interview with the advisory committee was the next morning at 8:00 a.m. The interview with the full board lasted three hours, and
included a brief interview with my wife, Judy. I was quite pleased with the
board interview. I began by making a personal statement, which had not

been part of the anticipated agenda, to emphasize that I thought I was ready to be president of Baylor, more so than I was six months ago. The basic reason was simply that in the intervening months I had thought extensively about the matter, and in that process had been able to be fully confident I could do the job.

There were a lot of questions that I was asked, and I thought I handled them all very well. For example, when asked about my capacity and likely success in working with donors, I remember saying specifically that I did not think fund-raising was "rocket science," that it really began with "friend raising," and I was good at that. I had to be careful on this point, since President Reynolds was in the room listening to every word I said, and he was considered an excellent fund-raiser. But I was comfortable with my response, and there was certainly no negative feedback.

The only point of negativity arose with a question about Baylor's longstanding policy regarding the prohibition of student dancing on campus. The question came from Hal Wingo, the editor of *People Magazine*. I quickly gathered that Wingo was unhappy and even embarrassed about our policy, since it was a widely shared means by which some of our detractors poked fun at "old Baptist Baylor." I responded by saying that if the Board of Regents gave the orders to drop the policy, I would be happy to oblige. After all, I had danced for years. I noted to the board that my wife actually taught me and I had no personal objection by any means. But I was aware that there were some in the room who still liked the policy, so I appealed to a *Newsweek* column by the conservative commentator, George Will, who had recently written about some institutional practices that, though "quaint" (his word), are valuable just for that reason. I likened our dancing policy to such a practice. While I thought I had made an interesting point, Wingo was aghast at what I said, perhaps especially because I had quoted George Will.

As I said, I was pleased with the interview and had no regrets about what I said, including my reference to George Will. When Judy and I got home that evening, I received a phone call from my brother, Edward, who was then associate executive director of the Baptist General Convention of Texas. In response to his asking me, "How did it go?" my reply was straightforward: "Ed, I felt like I was the president of Baylor for three hours." But that feeling for a brief three hours was all it would be! The next day the board selected Robert Sloan as the new president. Because of my current role as provost and chief academic officer, Sloan's appointment had an ironic twist for me. In his position as dean of Truett Seminary, Sloan reported to me. Now, in just a few months, I would be reporting to him.

Of all the other candidates' visions for Baylor, I assumed that Sloan's was probably closest to mine. In addition, Sloan had charm, statewide visibility, and intelligence, not to mention clear support within the Board of Regents. It became very evident to me later that during the search and interview process my candidacy never got traction. The inside dynamics, politics, and thinking of the board took matters in another direction. Though I had been confident in my candidacy for president, I was assured that even in this, God's providence was at work.

# 8

# THE SLOAN PRESIDENCY
## First Years

---

By all accounts, Herbert Reynolds and Robert Sloan had a strong professional relationship, if not a personal one. President Reynolds was responsible, more than any other individual, for the founding of Truett Theological Seminary at Baylor, and he singlehandedly was responsible for naming Robert Sloan as founding dean. Even though the dean of Truett would report to me as chief academic officer, Reynolds did not consult with me about the Sloan appointment. Reynolds had a high estimation of Sloan, that Sloan would be the "stack pole" around whom we would build the Truett faculty. As for Sloan, the respect was mutual. Sloan's significant respect for President Reynolds was illustrated by his refusal to refer to Reynolds in any other way than "President Reynolds" or "Dr. Reynolds." It was, in fact, a conviction I shared.

When the search for the new president began, no one, at least to my knowledge, was promoting a Sloan presidency. After all, he was only in his first year as dean of Truett, a unit with a handful of faculty and a total of fifty students, and had no other senior administrative experience. Furthermore, he was not interviewed by the search committee in its work during the summer and fall of 1994 to my knowledge. Sloan, in a sense, was an accidental president. I don't believe he had thought about the Baylor presidency very much until January of 1995 when he reached out to others for advice and counsel, in particular Clif Williams, a consultant to President Reynolds at the time and a close personal friend of mine.

Sloan asked for a meeting with me on March 9, 1995. We met in his small office at the First Baptist Church of Waco, where Truett Seminary was then located. At my invitation, we had met prior to the board's decision simply to offer mutual support, regardless what happened. At this second meeting, however, it was clear he was now the president-elect, and offered no assurances of any kind regarding my position. In fact, I detected a kind of firmness in his demeanor, particularly when he said, "It's all about faith and learning." Sloan seemed to say this with gripped fists, as though he knew he would have a fight on his hands with many in the Baylor community. My reaction was twofold: on the one hand, this vision was precisely my vision, hence I was very pleased. However, on the other hand, the way he said it worried me because I wondered if he doubted my commitment to this vision. I also wondered what other priorities he might have as the new Baylor president. No president can be so singularly focused.

The first day of Sloan's presidency was June 1, 1995. On that day he invited everyone at Baylor, but especially all staff members and administrators, to join him early in the afternoon in the Drawing Room of the Bill Daniel Student Center. There he was warmly greeted by a large gathered crowd, to wish him well and to hear what he would have to say on the first day of his presidency. He did not speak long, and, as I recall, offered no agenda of any substance. The one point I remember very well was his encouragement to everyone, "Just keep doing what you've been doing." It appeared to me that President Sloan wanted more than anything else to have a smooth transition from the presidency of Dr. Reynolds to his.

In July 1995, my wife and I, accompanied by John and Ruth Belew, travelled to Oxford for vacation time and Baylor business. The Baylor business part focused on relationships we were pursuing with a couple of Oxford colleges, one of which was Westminster. We were staying in a quite nice dormitory on the Westminster campus, when one afternoon, as I was walking through the lobby by the front desk area of the dorm, a phone call came through from Robert Sloan. He was calling from Harvard where he was attending a week-long seminar for new presidents, sponsored by the Institute for Educational Management. It was about 9:00 a.m. at Harvard, about 2:00 p.m. at Oxford.

He was catching up on "paper work" that he had brought with him, when he came across a Baylor institutional form for the replacement of a faculty member in the religion department, signed by the department chair, Glenn Hilburn; the dean of the College of Arts and Sciences, Bill Cooper; and me. The faculty member to be replaced was Alan Culpepper, a distinguished New Testament professor who had just accepted the deanship at the newly established divinity school at Mercer University. The procedure we were following for this replacement of a tenure-track faculty member was precisely what we had been following for years.

I quickly realized that Robert—we called each other by our first names—was not happy at all that he had not been consulted about this replacement action. Although I was completely shocked and puzzled by his reaction, we agreed we would discuss the matter when I returned from Oxford in another week or so. What I soon learned (although I had some inkling of this before) was that Robert Sloan had very mixed views about Baylor's religion department, and that he had lived and worked in tension with some of the members for years. The tension was not so much personal as it was theological. For example, he had battled other members of the department over some of the faculty hires who had been recruited. It was also the case, as best I understood, that Sloan had a more orthodox theology than most other members of the department.

The phone-call incident put me on alert regarding my relationship with Robert Sloan. I could take nothing for granted. While still at Oxford, I contacted my administrative assistant, who was then Beverly Locklin, instructing her to arrange weekly meetings between Sloan and me. I knew instinctively that if my relationship with Robert Sloan was going to work, I needed to take the initiative. We had these regular meetings for years, along with a number of "vice presidents' retreats" which enabled me to get to know my new boss.

During Robert Sloan's first year as president, most of the top members of the administrative team remained in place except for Bob Feather, vice president for development. Feather retired and was replaced by Gwin Morris, the associate vice president for development. The other change was the addition of Clif Williams in a new administrative position: vice president for human resources. Clif Williams was Sloan's chief confidant at this point. Their offices were adjacent and Sloan consulted with Clif on a wide range of issues, or so it appeared to me. At this time, I was definitely on the "outside" looking in.

By the spring semester of 1996, I had become concerned by some of the developments that were taking place at the senior administrative level. One was the firing of Gwin Morris after only about eight months as vice president for development. He was replaced by Richard Scott, long-time dean of the Hankamer School of Business. Richard reported to me for six years, but he didn't report to me in practice. He was very independent, more so than any of the other deans, but he was effective and he was a conservative Baptist. He could also raise money. Sloan definitely liked these qualities. Not surprisingly, Richard's appointment met with widespread approval, including from me. The concern I had was that Richard would have a disproportionate amount of influence with Sloan, and he wouldn't be reluctant to use it, including in the academic area.

The next administrative change was the departure of James Netherton, vice president of finance and administration and a protégé of Herbert Reynolds. Jim let me know privately that because he did not feel wanted by the new president, he began to pursue other options, including the provost position of Samford University. Jim was named to that position by May 1996, and left Baylor over the summer. When Jim left, he was replaced by Clif Williams who, in turn, was replaced as vice president for human resources by Marilyn Crone, a local banker and another conservative Baptist. One other significant change in 1996 was the departure of Mike Bishop as vice president for university marketing. Stan Madden, professor of marketing in the Hankamer School of Business and a long-time associate of Sloan's, was appointed to be Bishop's replacement. Now all of the vice presidents from the Reynolds administration were now gone except for Bill Hillis and me.

While I did not think President Sloan was hoping I would leave Baylor, I certainly did sense that I was being observed with a wary eye. This came through in a number of ways, but most especially in the faculty evaluation process and in the appointment of new deans. During the summer of 1995, Bill Cooper announced his intention to step down as dean of the College of Arts and Sciences by June 1996. The first task I faced, in collaboration with Sloan, was naming a search committee to seek Cooper's replacement. We began work on the naming of the committee in September. Because of Sloan's deep concern that we name a committee that would produce candidates who were just right for Baylor and acceptable to the new president, it took us six weeks to accomplish this seemingly straightforward job. As best I could tell, what Sloan was looking for in a new dean of the college was a traditional academic, one who would rein in the college's budget, and one who was a serious Christian, preferably a Baptist. Although I announced the final composition of the committee, the committee was actually more his than mine. He had micromanaged the entire process.

A second example related to personnel issues in the English department, issues arising out of questions of personal conduct. President Sloan took great interest in these matters in large part, I think, because he was convinced, as I was but not to the same degree, that the Baylor culture had become overly permissive regarding the personal conduct of faculty members and administrators. That needed to be stopped, he believed, and the best way to stop it was for the administration to be firm in applying our personnel policies. As to the English department episode, the final result was that a few people lost their positions and in some cases were dismissed from the university altogether.

I worried more and more about the Sloan presidency through the summer of 1996. In August of that year, I had to have emergency hernia surgery, and although the surgery was on an out-patient basis, the recovery period was an extremely painful one, lasting about five days at home. During these days, I thought a lot about the Baylor situation and what overall seemed to be the direction Sloan was taking Baylor. I wrote out notes to myself to gain some clarity in my own mind, and I knew I needed to talk with Clif Williams about my concerns.

On August 17, 1996, on the eve of my fifty-sixth birthday, Clif and his wife, Jan, and Jim and Betsy Vardaman, all mutual friends, came to our home for dinner and conversation. After dinner, I pulled out my notes and went over them with Clif, though the others listened in with considerable interest. The two parts of my discussion notes, which I saved and later titled "A Discussion with Clif Williams at Home," revealed my strong feelings and concerns:

1. A definite rightward direction overall, ideologically and operationally

   —our capacity to be a real university is in question;

   —rigidity in hiring and other personnel decisions;

   —no big ideas—hold the course;

   —hunker down on finances. The main target has become the academic program, especially the college.

2. An anti-faculty sentiment is emerging

—negative personnel decisions;

—lack of trust in many faculty members;

—lack of trust in the faculty senate;

—greater stress on research but no flexibility on approaches to faculty loads.

My notes concluded with these thoughts: "I am not the chief academic officer. Very short leash: search committees, appointments, faculty hires, routine stuff. I'm hemmed in almost regardless of what I do. I don't feel trusted. I am largely isolated. I'm not looked to for my ideas or counsel."

These were difficult matters for me to bring up with Clif. At this time he was very devoted to Sloan's presidency and to him personally, and although I thought that my concerns would get a somewhat sympathetic hearing from him, he actually defended President Sloan on almost every point. I was a bit surprised, but we had a fruitful discussion and I knew Clif would keep our discussion in confidence. Moreover, perhaps he would have some influence with Sloan on my behalf.

In spite of my worries about Baylor's direction under Sloan, I was not in a desperate state of mind regarding my job security. The president of Mercer University, Kirby Godsey, whom I had known for several years, called me in late August to ask if I would be willing to consider the position of executive vice president and provost at Mercer. I said I would be, and following that initial contact, I had three productive and encouraging meetings with Godsey, including visits with him, the top vice presidents, and others at the Mercer campus in Macon, Georgia. For the second visit, Judy accompanied me, and one of our major goals was to find a house where we might live in the Macon area. During a third visit, Judy and I were invited to meet with several distinguished Mercer supporters and alumni for dinner in a downtown Atlanta hotel. The group included the chair of the Mercer board as well as the governor of Georgia.

I told one of my long-time friends from North Carolina, Bob Mullinax, upon his visit to our home in Waco in the fall of 1996, that I thought chances were very high that I would be moving to Mercer. However, the momentum for this move—and the naming of Mercer's provost—was put on hold because of a controversial book by Godsey published in the fall of 1996, entitled *When We Talk About God, Let's Be Honest*. The book brought enormous attention to Godsey, most of it negative, and caused a furor for him in Georgia and elsewhere. He was quite distracted by the controversy, which took his mind away from such matters as choosing a new provost. This delay at Mercer led me to think more deeply about my future at Baylor.

On February 7, 1997, I wrote a letter to Godsey withdrawing my name from any further consideration for the position at Mercer. I elaborated as follows:

> During the last several weeks I have had the opportunity, fortuitous perhaps, to think hard and long about my situation. For reasons not entirely clear to me, my relationship with Robert Sloan has noticeably improved. I think time is one factor. Perhaps the real prospect that I might leave is another. I have observed that he seems more comfortable with me and has demonstrated more confidence in me. I have also been strongly encouraged by a lot of people at Baylor to stay. Naturally, that has had an impact on me. And . . . I have found myself losing interest in the position at Mercer.
>
> Robert Sloan and I had a long conversation about all these matters yesterday. I concluded by telling him that it is definitely my preference to stay at Baylor. He was genuinely pleased to hear that, commenting at some length on why. I have had increasing reason to believe this would be his response. In any case, I am fully satisfied that he wants me to be his chief academic officer and the Provost at Baylor.

One significant piece of information that Sloan discussed with me that day was the fact, totally unknown to me previously, that he had signed the necessary legal papers for me to assume the presidency, on an interim basis, were anything to happen to him such that he would be unable to perform the duties of the office. That information certainly got my attention.

Another bit of heartening news was a letter to President Sloan, sent on March 26, 1997, from the ten academic deans of Baylor. I had always had a strong working relationship with these deans both individually and collectively. In addition, we were friends at a personal level, as were all of our spouses. Out of their concern regarding the rumors of my possible departure to Mercer, the deans decided to communicate with President Sloan to indicate their strong support for my staying at Baylor. Here is the essence of the letter, addressed to Sloan, a copy of which I received and initialed on March 27, 1997:

> Recently, Dr. Schmeltekopf was under consideration for the position of Provost at Mercer University. As the deans of the schools and academic units of the University, we individually expressed

our concern to Dr. Schmeltekopf over the prospect that he would leave his position as Provost at Baylor.

Our concern was prompted by a plain observation: while we have worked closely with Dr. Schmeltekopf for varying periods of decanal service, we uniformly respect and admire his leadership and service as Provost. He has allowed each of us appropriate freedom of judgment and action in regard to our respective academic units, while concurrently providing strong and directed leadership toward our common goals. Put simply, he has in his leadership fostered the best of both ideal and practice in fulfilling the aims of Baylor as a modern university.

Dr. Schmeltekopf has advised us of his decision to withdraw from consideration for the position at Mercer. His decision was met with uniform accolade by us. Those of us who have spoken to you regarding Dr. Schmeltekopf's candidacy at Mercer are aware that you share our assessment of, and appreciation for, Dr. Schmeltekopf's academic leadership at Baylor as Provost.

The letter was signed by all ten of the deans. I happened to know that Brad Toben, dean of the School of Law, was the organizer of this effort and the letter was written on School of Law letterhead, Office of the Dean. No one at Baylor was more supportive of my work than Dean Toben; he was rock solid. It is an interesting fact that both he and I began in our respective positions at Baylor in 1991.

When I became the provost at Baylor in 1991, the position was not a particularly strong one. The deans and the president were the main decision-makers at the administrative level. This was not unique to Baylor, however; it was largely the case across most of higher education in the United States until after World War II, when the great influx of new students created more of a demand for a chief academic officer other than the president and when the desire for a corporate form of management began to take hold in universities on a wide scale. In fact, the position of provost did not exist in most universities prior to this time period. Even Harvard did not have a permanent provost until 1993.

The legacy of the president being the chief academic officer, with deans reporting directly to the president, was a legacy I was dealing with at Baylor, under both President Reynolds and President Sloan. The role of the dean, unlike that of the provost, was a very familiar position. A dean was the head of a particular faculty and had real power both because of that fact and because all the deans had significant budgets. The provost, on the other hand, did not have a specific faculty and, as I have previously noted in my own case, virtually no budget for several years. So, I adopted the view—privately held—that the deans were "my faculty." When non-academic people would frequently ask me, "What is a provost?" my meant-for-humor answer was often, "the keeper of the prison," which is actually one of the historical meanings of the word "provost." As chief academic officer and provost, one of my goals was to elevate the status and overall influence of the position of provost within the Baylor community. I think I succeeded.

My work as provost was seriously complicated in 1997 when President Sloan decided that he wanted to have a direct role in the interviews of prospective faculty members, which had not been the practice at Baylor except for new hires in the religion department. One of the main reasons was practical—presumably there was not enough time in the day for the president of a major university to be interviewing all candidates for faculty positions. At Baylor, we interviewed over one hundred every year. The president had more important things to do, such as overseeing the entire university and developing relationships with regents, alumni, political, religious, and community leaders, and perhaps most importantly, prospective donors. President Sloan understood that, but in his third year as president, he was convinced that building a certain kind of faculty was more important than anything else. It became clear that even though I was the chief academic officer on paper, he was the chief academic officer in reality, at least with respect to faculty hiring.

Initially I was concerned about this arrangement; I wondered if it would work, both on our side of the table and the candidates' side of the table. But I must confess, it did! All the deans and I found ourselves in accord with President Sloan regarding the qualifications of new faculty members to be hired at Baylor. The qualifications we really cared about were a combination of academic, religious, and personal ones. All faculty interviews at the administrative level were held in one of the conference rooms in Pat Neff Hall, and there we—Sloan, me, the respective dean, perhaps the department chair—met with each candidate for about forty minutes. My key administrative assistant, Paulette Edwards, somehow managed to get us all together at the same time and in the same place. In addition, all of us had received in advance a candidate file that contained several documents, including a letter of application, curriculum vitae, letters of recommendation, and a form indicating information about church/denominational affiliation.

All the interviews were structured similarly. After introductions, I would begin the discussion by asking the candidate to tell the assembled group a little about his or her background, such as where the candidate was from, his or her key experiences in life, and his or her religious history. The last-mentioned usually opened the door for an extended give-and-take about Baylor's Christian mission and how the candidate might contribute to that mission. In addition, and in the most sensitive way possible yet unapologetically, we wanted to get some insight into whether the candidate embraced the historic teachings of the Christian faith, or as we would put it to ourselves, was within the "big tent of orthodox Christianity." Then the dean would generally move the discussion to matters of scholarly and teaching interests. This part of the conversation was central to the administrative interview, even though none of us, perhaps, had academic expertise in the candidate's discipline. But we wanted to be sure we saw a passion for both scholarly work and the intellectual and personal challenge of teaching. President Sloan was always the last to raise questions with the candidate, and he was particularly adept at playing off what had already been spoken by the candidate. This regular format of faculty interviews helped me understand Sloan's religious and intellectual perspectives in a wider way than ever before.

President Sloan participated in these administrative interviews of prospective faculty members for three years. In retrospect, I can say this: During the four years I served as provost under President Reynolds, I was personally responsible for rejecting only one faculty candidate who came through the recruiting system—that is, from the department, to the dean, and then to the provost and the president. President Reynolds supported my negative decision regarding the candidate, but because he was concerned that we handle the matter properly with the department in question, he called a meeting, in his office, of the department chair, the dean, and me to discuss the situation. I argued that the proposed hire was simply not a good fit for Baylor on several levels, although the candidate had just received a PhD from an Ivy League school. In the end, everyone agreed that we should continue the search, and we did. The individual finally selected from that search remains at Baylor to this day.

During the Sloan administration, however, it was not particularly unusual for faculty candidates to be rejected at the administrative level. Not surprisingly, this caused considerable consternation initially with many faculty members. But over time, with the help of the deans and department chairs, most faculty members came to accept the higher standards for faculty hiring, particularly with respect to religious questions, being imposed by the administration. One piece of evidence that speaks to this was the adoption of a religious affiliation form, endorsed by the Faculty Senate in 1998, that required information about the candidate's church affiliation provided by the department chair or the relevant dean. (This information usually was gathered by a phone call with the candidate or from a letter the candidate submitted.) The form also provided space for me, as provost, to enter my own assessment, after the administrative interview, of the candidate's level of church involvement and/or Christian commitment. This completed form was then made a part of the official file of the candidate.

This targeted emphasis on faculty hiring, especially as it related to the religious component, was probably the single most important factor in the growing seriousness of Baylor as a Christian university. This definitely was a change from earlier decades when it was assumed that the profile of faculty recruits would reflect Baylor's Baptist tradition and an acceptance of a certain religious culture at Baylor. But beginning in the 1960s, with the widespread secularization of American culture and especially of virtually all the major graduate schools in the country, very little could now be assumed about the Christian commitment of our candidates, including Baptist ones. If Baylor was to avoid going the direction, from a religious standpoint, of universities such as Vanderbilt and Wake Forest, we had to be very intentional about hiring faculty members who really cared about the Christian faith and Baylor's Christian mission.

This targeted effort corresponded perfectly with our emphasis on faith and learning. Indeed, the faith/learning project represented a fresh way at Baylor to define the essence of a Christian university—that is, thinking Christianly about human life and the world. Although we didn't expect all new faculty members to have a considered view on the matter, we certainly wanted them to be willing to think about the implications for connecting their Christian faith to academic life and to their own scholarly work. As I said in my speech to the Board of Regents in 1992, "in a Christian university, the members of the chemistry department and the math department, and those in other quantitative and scientific [and professional] fields, as well as the humanities and the arts, ought to be a part of a larger learning community." And then I added these words: "Encouraging this kind of learning community at Baylor is what I see now as my most important task as chief academic officer."

We not only hired to the Christian mission of Baylor, but we also devoted time and resources to faculty development, both for new faculty members as well as current ones. This was a key to encouraging the kind of learning community I described to the board. A new faculty orientation seminar, sponsored and funded by the provost's office, was co-directed by Dianna Vitanza, vice provost for academic affairs, and Mike Beaty, director of the Institute for Faith and Learning. The seminar, held over four days prior to the beginning of the fall semester, included a variety of sessions, many of which brought in speakers from our own faculty and from other Christian colleges and universities. On the final evening of the program, all participants and their spouses were invited to the Schmeltekopf home on the Brazos River for a barbeque dinner—in the back yard overlooking the river. Additionally, all the participants were compensated $1000 each for their attendance at the seminar. We averaged about thirty-five new faculty members per year; they all came.

I have called this chapter "The Sloan Presidency: First Years" for a good reason. The first year or so was a period of uncertainty for me, but by the end of 1997, matters were clearer. At that point, other important developments came into play, and none more important than scholarship and graduate education.

## AN EXCURSUS: THE INSTITUTE FOR FAITH AND LEARNING

As I discussed in chapter 2, "Early Initiatives," the advocacy of faith and learning, as an integrated unity, was high on my list of intellectual goals at Baylor. My commitment to this goal was based on the notion that a serious Christian university should be distinguishable in important ways from the typical secular university of the twentieth and twenty-first centuries. Somehow, religious truth—that Jesus Christ is Lord; that all truth is God's truth—should inform the core identity of Baylor. As difficult as these notions may be for the secular-inclined mind to fathom, we nevertheless should always seek to understand their meaning within our context. Hence, my creation of faith and learning discussion groups for the first five years of my work as the chief academic officer.

Two years into the Sloan administration marked a propitious time to embed the faith/learning project in a permanent way into Baylor's structure. Thus, in 1997 we created the Institute for Faith and Learning, with Mike Beaty, my early conversation partner on the topic of faith and learning, as its first director. The mission of the institute was to help Baylor achieve its goal and vision of being the premier Protestant/Christian university in the United States. Since its founding, the institute has developed several programs in support of this mission, including especially faculty development opportunities, such as the new faculty orientation seminar mentioned above, the cultivation of high-quality research among faculty, the mentoring of students, the encouragement of teaching that is faithful to the Christian intellectual tradition, and the sponsorship of a major annual conference.

With regard to the latter, I organized and sponsored the first of these conferences in the spring of 1996 under the name, "The Baylor Symposium." The theme of this first conference, appropriately enough, was "Faith and Learning," and the theme of the second conference, held in 1997, was "Health Care and the Church." These were two-day conferences that drew academics and laity alike from both within and outside Baylor. In 1998 the Baylor Symposium was absorbed into the work of the institute, and soon came under the name, "The Pruitt Symposium," in honor of the family of Ella and Levi Pritchard, who provided a significant endowment to support the conference.

In 2002, Mike Beaty was succeeded as director by Doug Henry, another Christian philosopher. Henry served as director until 2008 when he was succeeded by Darin Davis, yet another Christian philosopher.

Today the Institute for Faith and Learning is a fixture within the work of Baylor. It is well funded by the university, has several staff members, and makes just the kind of contribution to Baylor's mission as a Christian research university that is needed. The institute also, and importantly, has gained wide support within the university community. One piece of evidence of this is the fact that the director reports directly to the provost, giving him access to the top leadership of Baylor. Another bit of evidence is the prestige of the annual conference, now under the heading, "The Baylor Symposium on Faith and Culture," a three-day event that draws an attendance of 400 annually, many of whom are students from other Baptist and Christian universities. The keynote speakers are outstanding Christian scholars of national reputations. No other academic event at Baylor, other than our commencements, has this level of visibility. Indeed, our program on faith and learning has become a model for Christian colleges and universities across the country.

# 9

# A NEW DAY FOR SCHOLARSHIP AND GRADUATE EDUCATION

———————————

The responsibilities of faculty members at Baylor had always been focused on teaching and the mentoring of and care for students. The university's official Faculty Workload Policy, adopted in 1958 when Baylor moved from the quarter system to the semester system, required a teaching load of twelve hours each semester or twenty-four hours for the academic year. Within this teaching-intensive environment, however, faculty responsibilities in the area of scholarship had been increasing over the decades in certain academic areas, such as departments with doctoral programs as well as in the Hankamer School of Business, prompted by partially endowed professorships. In fact, by the mid-1990s, more and more faculty members were hired on the condition that they pursue an active research agenda.

Early in President Sloan's administration, it became increasingly clear that the faculty workload policy needed to be reexamined to reflect current practices more accurately. Some of the academic deans in particular were lobbying to make research no longer optional but required. The question was, however, required for whom? For the traditional faculty members who had full teaching loads for years and who were really in no position to undertake a serious research agenda at this point in their careers? No, the change would apply to faculty members who had active roles in graduate programs, who were engaged in funded research, and to all recent and new hires who were brought to Baylor with the expectation that they would be productive, publishing scholars.

A new policy on faculty responsibilities was approved first in September 1997, and then slightly revised and reissued on February 4, 1998. The policy was unanimously recommended by the Council of Deans, which at the time included the chair of the Faculty Senate, and then forwarded to me and the president for final approval. Named the "Statement on Scholarly Expectations at Baylor University," its key elements are as follows:

> Baylor University has always placed a very high value on schol-arly teaching, and this commitment remains unchanged. More recently, the University has increasingly emphasized the impor-tance of other forms of scholarly activity as a means of advancing the University's mission. Such activity broadly defined includes 1) traditional forms of research resulting in discoveries that are pub-licly disseminated, 2) reflection that creatively integrates ideas, 3) creative performances and productions typically associated with the fine arts, 4) the application of knowledge in solving problems, and 5) research, writings, and presentations that focus on the activity of teaching itself. . . . University expectations regarding the types of scholarly activity will necessarily vary depending on available resources, the goals and objectives of the various schools and departments, and the diversity of contributions made to the University by individual faculty members.

This new policy reflected the then-current realities at Baylor as more and more faculty members were already being hired with the expectation that they would be engaged in scholarly activity, publically disseminated, in addition to teaching. As a result, the new policy came as no surprise and, in fact, was embraced broadly throughout the university community, including in promotion and tenure decisions. These changes were not made overnight, but incrementally over a period of three or four years. By 1998 the traditional teaching load of twelve hours per semester was essentially abandoned for those faculty members who were engaged in serious re-search activities. This meant, among other things, that we were adding new faculty members at a level never before experienced at Baylor.

Alongside the increased emphasis on scholarship was a growing awareness at Baylor by the mid-1990s that we needed to be much more involved in graduate education. Not only was this the view of many faculty members and various academic units, but it was also a realization reflected in the work of the Sesquicentennial Council of 150 (see chapter 5) and by our membership in the Big XII (see chapter 4; Baylor was the only member school not classified as a research university). However, when Robert Sloan first became president in June 1995, it seemed that the momentum for increased graduate work at Baylor might be reversed, that we would revert to being a one-dimensional university, a large undergraduate school combined with a relatively small, albeit prominent, law school. This observation is based largely on President Sloan's public comments in which he stressed repeatedly the overriding importance of our undergraduate mission. In fact, in those first years Sloan rarely mentioned graduate education at all.

Perhaps one factor at play in this regard was President Sloan's uncertainty about the dean of the Graduate School, Henry Walbesser. Dr. Walbesser became dean in 1992 and quickly pursued a very aggressive course in the growth of the Graduate School, both in number of students and overall programs, including new PhD programs. A problem developed, however, and during the fall semester of 1996, Dean Walbesser made some disparaging comments about President Sloan that reached our Waco newspaper, the *Tribune-Herald*. Shortly thereafter, Walbesser was removed from his position of graduate dean and replaced on an interim basis by the associate dean, Darden Powers.

I knew immediately that graduate education would be seen with a more favorable eye by Sloan than was previously the case. Dr. Powers was a highly respected and long-time professor of physics at Baylor, serving as chair of the department for several years. He had sterling credentials, holding a PhD from Cal Tech, and he was a conservative and active Baptist Christian. He had been a finalist for the deanship when Walbesser was selected, but the search committee recommended Dr. Walbesser, who of course had many assets himself.

One of the first things we did after Dr. Powers was named acting dean was to develop a "Position Paper for the Baylor Graduate School." This position paper was issued as a report of the Academic Task Force of the University Planning Council, a body created shortly after Sloan was named president. The task force included department chairs and deans, including Dean Wallace Daniel of the College of Arts and Sciences, Dean Phyllis Karns of the School of Nursing, and Darden Powers himself. I served as chair, but perhaps the most important member was Larry Lyon, professor of sociology and acting associate dean of the graduate school, who led in the conceptualization and drafting of the position paper. Dr. Lyon was deeply committed to graduate education and shared my concern about its uncertain direction at Baylor under the new presidency of Robert Sloan. In addition, he and I were both alarmed by the ranking of Baylor's doctoral programs by the National Research Council and by Baylor's standing in the Big XII as the only member not classified as a research university.

While the position paper acknowledged the relative progress of the Graduate School during the mid-1990s, the report contained plenty of bad news about the state of graduate work at Baylor and about the institutional conditions necessary for graduate education to thrive. For example, Baylor offered only fourteen doctoral programs, the lowest by far of any of the Big XII institutions. (By contrast, Texas A&M offered seventy-five.) As reported in 1995, Baylor's overall student-faculty ratio was 21:1, which meant that most faculty members involved in graduate education were also responsible for a significant number of undergraduate students. The same report indicated a low level of external funding per Baylor faculty member—$1,815—an amount substantially below all other universities in the comparison group. But perhaps the most devastating news was that of all the doctoral programs at Baylor, only the religion program was ranked even in the top half of all listed doctoral programs in the country, according to the National Research Council's report of 1995.

Most faculty members involved in graduate education at Baylor were generally aware of these matters. In truth, as Robert Collmer told me in 1991 when I met with him as the dean of the Graduate School, Baylor was doing graduate education "on the cheap." That Baylor had a graduate program at all was due largely to the good will and effort of interested faculty members and departments. But, the position paper asked, what about the future? Did Baylor have the resources and the determination to move to a higher level in graduate education and research? What was needed at this point, declared the position paper, was a "vision [that] will define the goals for graduate and professional education at Baylor . . . and a strategic plan [that] can outline the steps that will help us reach those goals." With a vision and strategic plan articulated, maybe George Marsden's notion of "Christian graduate studies," as described in chapter 3, could be realized at Baylor after all.

The vision expressed by the position paper was straightforward: Build a graduate program at Baylor that would enhance our mission as adopted by the faculty and Board of Regents in 1994—excellence in undergraduate, professional, and graduate education—and move the university forward in becoming a preeminent Christian university. This vision was followed by six criteria designed to be the means by which the vision might be realized:

1. Graduate programs must emphasize quality more than quantity, and quality graduate programs can and should enhance the quality of undergraduate programs.

2. The doctoral offerings should increase sufficiently to allow the university to secure and maintain a strong Doctoral Division I status with the Carnegie Classifications. [We were Division II at the time.]

3. Graduate programs might be expected to have some relevance to the Christian character of the university . . . . Baylor should emphasize that it has an uncommon and valuable combination in graduate and professional education—high quality academics combined with a setting harmonious with the Christian faith.

4. Baylor's graduate programs should be of high academic quality or at least making demonstrable progress in that direction.

5. New graduate programs should be required to demonstrate that they can achieve academic excellence without significantly reducing the resources available to existing graduate programs.

6. Graduate programs should be both faculty-centered and student-centered. Programs must demonstrate . . . that students are adequately prepared for and able to secure employment.

The position paper was endorsed by most faculty members, the Council of Deans, and the administration, as well as the academic affairs committee of the Board of Regents, and became the operating plan for graduate education by the Sloan administration by the summer of 1998. And, importantly, Larry Lyon was named the new dean of the Graduate School. Probably for the first time in its history, Baylor now had in place a real commitment to graduate education, a vision and plan to give it direction, and a dean who not only could be an effective leader but who also had the strong support of the top administration. No stronger evidence for the success of this new emphasis on graduate education can be given than that today Baylor is designated as a research university by the Carnegie Foundation, our doctoral graduates are being hired widely and many by Christian colleges and universities, and Larry Lyon remains the dean of the Graduate School.

## REFLECTIONS

I served as chief academic officer in two Baylor administrations over a span of twelve years, four with President Reynolds and eight with President Sloan. Under these administrations, there were both continuities and discontinuities regarding policy matters. The greatest discontinuity had to do with the commitment to and funding of research and graduate education. Reynolds was certainly committed to research and graduate education, but he was very conservative about making these an institutional priority when it came to funding. As I have already mentioned, the matter of graduate education never came up in my interviews with the search committee or in my early discussions with Reynolds about my agenda as the new chief academic officer. Graduate education was simply not an institutional priority. In 1992 I discussed with Jim Netherton, the vice president for finance and administration, the need for a blue-ribbon committee to review and clarify Baylor's role in graduate education. He did not support the idea at all, and while he did not say as much, I assume that his negative reaction was primarily about funding. Netherton knew Reynolds's mind on financial matters.

At least annually President Reynolds would discuss with me his concern about the excessive amount of released time given to faculty members and its cost to the university. Reynolds calculated precisely the released time—regardless the reason—per each faculty member and pointed out that a reduction of released time would save the university tens of thousands of dollars. I faithfully passed along Reynolds's concern to the deans, but the problem was that the overwhelming majority of the released time was for administrative purposes in the academic division, such as for department chairs, division heads, deans, associate deans, and special program heads. Because academic administrative management was simply an operational necessity, released time at Baylor during Reynolds's administration could not be reduced at all.

Correlative to this perspective was Reynolds's reluctance to support high salaries for specific faculty or administrative positions. This made it difficult to recruit distinguished faculty members around whom to build excellent graduate programs, but this matter was also and perhaps especially, restricting in the hiring of coaches, particularly in football and basketball. As chief academic officer, I had nothing to do with athletics, of course, other than to be an informed supporter. But Reynolds's principle was that no one should make more than the president, and in the age of high-profile college sports, that principle, though noble, would prove to be self-defeating.

Understandably, President Sloan started out his administration essentially holding to the same views regarding the funding of research and graduate education, as well as salaries for some specific positions, both faculty and coaches. By the end of his third year, however, his views had changed. Perhaps one explanation had to do with the hiring of Harold Cunningham, a member of the Board of Regents and one who knew a thing or two about money, as the vice president for finance and administration. But I'm sure Sloan's more liberal perspective was simply a result of three years of presidential experience. In any case, under President Sloan, the support for faculty research and the expansion of the Graduate School became an institutional priority for the first time in school history. In addition, we soon launched an aggressive campaign to recruit nationally recognized scholars. In fact, I recall Sloan commenting to me regarding an exceptionally high salary—at least high for Baylor—we were offering one candidate for a distinguished faculty position, "Well, we pay coaches more than that." It turned out that salaries for coaches helped break the glass ceiling for some faculty salaries.

# 10

# UNIVERSITY AND
# DISTINGUISHED PROFESSORS

---

In my address to the Board of Regents in July of 1992 (see chapter 3), I emphasized that Notre Dame should be the model for Baylor in our attempt to become one of the foremost Christian universities in the country, if not the world. I went on to say that there would likely be considerable resistance among some in the Baylor community to such a proposal. I offered three strategies to overcome this possible resistance: the creation of a national commission to offer a plan for the future of Baylor; the enhancement of the Graduate School through an emphasis on Christian graduate studies; and the appointment of a number of "talented senior academic people" who would want to be a part of a university in which the Christian faith was vibrant. This latter suggestion came right out of Notre Dame's "Colloquy of the Year 2000," issued in 1990. In the colloquy report, one of Notre Dame's stated goals was to increase the total number of fully endowed chairs at the university by fifty over the following ten years.

The appointment of a number of "talented senior academic people" at Baylor was, in my opinion, a potentially groundbreaking idea. However, the proposal got no support at all from the development office, the president's office, or the regents. President Reynolds never commented to me on the idea at all, I think because fund raising at Baylor had been primarily for student scholarships or for the construction of new buildings. Yes, there were a number of endowed professorships, especially but not exclusively in the Hankamer School of Business, but virtually all of them were only partially funded. No more than a handful of fully funded endowed chairs existed in the entire university in the mid-1990s. Raising funds for additional distinguished positions may have seemed an insurmountable task not worthy of discussion.

By the summer of 1997, however, I was encouraged by my relationship with President Sloan and confident that I was now the real chief academic officer. Thus, I revisited my earlier proposal and moved forward on a bold, new initiative: university and distinguished professors. In addition to the Notre Dame model, an important motivation for these new faculty positions was the emerging vision, suggested initially by the Sesquicentennial Council of 150, that Baylor should be a "world class" university, indeed, one of the foremost universities of its kind anywhere. This vision came to be articulated in a few contexts in the first two years of the Sloan administration, including by the University Planning Council on June 6, 1996, when it declared that Baylor should become "the leading Christian university in the world."

As I have already indicated with respect to graduate education, there was a large gap between vision and reality. Yes, we could claim, honestly, that we were the only Protestant-affiliated, comprehensive, doctoral-granting university whose mission remained firmly rooted in its Christian community of origin, namely, Baptists. But we were not close to the academic standing of Catholic schools such as Notre Dame or Georgetown University. For example, Notre Dame was ranked by the *U.S. News & World Report* in the mid-1990s in the top twenty national undergraduate universities. Baylor was seventy-sixth. At the same time, Notre Dame had over eighty fully endowed professorships, and was seeking fifty more. Baylor had very few fully funded professorships, apart from the prestigious Robert Foster Cherry Professorship and the Chavanne Chair of Christian Ethics in Business, the latter of which I held for three years after my provostial service. These could be examples for others at Baylor, I thought, and focusing on their value to our community could pave the way for a new category of faculty scholar.

I approached President Sloan with the university and distinguished professors idea during one of our weekly meetings in early summer of 1997. I was uncertain what his response might be, particularly regarding the fund-raising part that, I assumed, would be necessary as well as the length of time needed to raise such funds, given the tradition of philanthropy at Baylor focusing on student scholarships and buildings. I proposed that we recruit one or two such professors on an annual basis until we reached twenty. After hearing me out, to my utter amazement and delight, he not only agreed and supported the initiative but offered to fund it from the operating budget. I had no idea that was within the realm of possibility, but Robert Sloan was not afraid of taking a big, albeit considered risk. President Reynolds's financial conservatism would not have supported this approach at all.

To proceed, we developed two documents with significant help from Institute for Faith and Learning director Mike Beaty, who composed the original drafts. In each document—one making the case for university professors and one for distinguished professors—we began with definitions. University professor "will be a rank awarded to a tenured full professor whose outstanding scholarship and national reputation for excellence in his or her academic areas of expertise transcend the bounds of traditional academic departments." We were interested here with the proven capacity of a scholar whose work demonstrated interdisciplinary and multidisciplinary implications. In contrast to this, distinguished professor "will be a rank awarded to a tenured full professor in a department or school/college of the University whose outstanding scholarship and national reputation for excellence in his or her academic discipline greatly exceeds the bounds of scholarship exemplified by most if not all other faculty members in that academic unit at Baylor." For both positions, we emphasized not only high achievement in scholarship widely recognized in the academy, but also a commitment to issues and themes central to Baylor's mission as a Christian university. Significantly, the compensation for both would be in the six-figure range, which was not insignificant at Baylor in 1997, especially in the College of Arts and Sciences.

We did not make a public announcement about the creation of the new university and distinguished professor faculty positions, although I had discussed the possibility with the deans and distributed both documents to them on November 18, 1997. (A clarification: In fact, there were already a few faculty members whose positions carried the name "distinguished," such as Bill Hillis in biology and Charles Talbert in religion. These were very limited in number and did not represent an institutional strategy.) The implementation of this new effort to enhance our faculty was left largely up to me as chief academic officer. My first priority was to recruit new faculty members from either religion or philosophy—or both. So, I contacted Glenn Hilburn, chair of the religion department, and Bob Baird, chair of the philosophy department, about our new program, and asked them individually if their respective departments would be interested in a new faculty position, one that would be "free," from a budget standpoint, and would not count against their allotment of tenured faculty positions. After conferring with the senior colleagues in their departments, they both agreed that they would be interested.

The religion department moved quickly in the fall semester of 1997 to bring forward a name for consideration: Ralph C. Wood, a professor of theology for twenty-six years at Wake Forest University and a former colleague of Charles Talbert. Wood was at the time on the faculty of Samford University, where he had just moved over the summer of 1997. Because it was proposed that he be given the title of University Professor of Theology and Literature, to reflect the interdisciplinary role of university professors, the English department would be involved in the appointment process as well. Professor Wood visited Baylor in late March 1998 for three days, during which time he was interviewed by a number of people in both departments, as well as by President Sloan and me. He also gave a public lecture in the Drawing Room of the Bill Daniel Student Center on Flannery O'Connor. The lecture and interviews went very well. We offered the position to Wood effective August 1998 and he accepted. To my great delight, over the years and to this day, Dr. Wood has been an ideal university professor for Baylor in precisely the way we designed the program.

Soon after the original contact was made with me by the religion department, the philosophy department, under Bob Baird's leadership, came forward with a recommendation for a Distinguished Professor of Philosophy: Carl Vaught, professor of philosophy at Penn State University. While some in the religion department knew Wood, everybody in the philosophy department knew Vaught. Not only was he a graduate of Baylor's philosophy department, but he also was brought in as a consultant to the department a couple of years prior to this time. As with Wood, Vaught gave a lecture and was interviewed by a number of people in the philosophy department and by President Sloan, Dean Wallace Daniel, and me. I had lunch with Professor Vaught and his wife on May 5, 1998, offering him the position, and he accepted on the spot. Our university and distinguished professor program was off to a great start by fall 1998: Ralph Wood and Carl Vaught, both stellar Christian scholars.

Over the next five years we named twelve additional university and distinguished professors:

- Marc H. Ellis (1999), University Professor of American and Jewish Studies

- David Lyle Jeffrey (2000), Distinguished Professor of Literature and Humanities

- Robert C. Roberts (2000), Distinguished Professor of Ethics

- C. Stephen Evans (2001), University Professor of Philosophy and Humanities

- Walter L. Bradley (2002), Distinguished Professor of Mechanical Engineering

- Stanley J. Grenz (2002), Distinguished Professor of Theology

- Johnny L. Henderson (2002), Distinguished Professor of Mathematics

- Thomas S. Hibbs (2003), Distinguished Professor of Ethics and Culture

- Robert Marks (2003), Distinguished Professor of Electrical and Computer Engineering

- Martin J. Medhurst (2003), Distinguished Professor of Rhetoric and Communication

- Bennie F. L. Ward (2003), Distinguished Professor of Physics

- Earl L. Grinols (2004, hired in 2003), Distinguished Professor of Economics

These appointments, along with Professors Wood and Vaught, were a remarkable addition to our faculty. They were all top scholars in their own right and all were serious Christians, except Marc Ellis, who was Jewish.

One element of the university and distinguished professors program was what I called the "Council of Scholars." The council met once each semester, beginning in the fall of 1998, primarily for the purpose of recommending prospective faculty members who might be particularly suitable for Baylor, including as university or distinguished professors. One such recommendation that came forward through the Council of Scholars was

David Lyle Jeffrey, who at the time was professor emeritus of the English department at the University of Ottawa. Ralph Wood made the initial contact with Jeffrey in October 1999, asking him if he would consider an appointment at Baylor as a university or distinguished professor. Soon after this initial contact, I was in conversation with Jeffrey to encourage him to consider Baylor and come to Waco for a visit as soon as could be arranged, which he did in February 2000, accompanied by his wife, Katherine.

It was a very profitable visit. Jeffrey met with a number of people in the English department, as well as President Sloan, Dean Daniel, and me, and gave a grand public lecture on C. S. Lewis in Bennett Auditorium to a packed audience. One particularly important event was a dinner in my home that included David and Katherine, and a few members of the English department, such as the chair Maurice Hunt, Jay Losey, who was a former student of Jeffrey's, and Jim LeMaster. One part of the dinner conversation that evening was extemporaneous statements by each faculty member on what Baylor meant to them, as a university in which to work and as a university with a distinctive mission. The Jeffreys were impressed.

Jeffrey accepted our offer and began his work at Baylor in August of 2000. David remains one of the most impressive scholars I have ever known in my career. Additionally, as a result of his wide range of personal and professional contacts, he was soon helping us with potential university and distinguished faculty members, as well as other faculty recruits. His extensive experience in higher education and his first-hand knowledge of Christian scholars led President Sloan and me to invite him into the provost's office as senior vice provost in the summer of 2001. Jeffrey was important in the recruitment of new faculty members to Baylor who would be excellent scholars and supportive of our mission as a Christian university.

## REFLECTIONS

Not everyone at Baylor embraced the university and distinguished faculty program. In fact, by 2005 such appointments had come to a halt. I was no longer provost at this time, but there seemed to be three main factors that contributed to this lack of continuing support. One was financial. Baylor had fallen on hard times by 2005 because of enrollment pressures brought on primarily by much higher levels of tuition costs to new students. Another was a change in priorities initiated by the new leadership of the university. The third was a backlash from some faculty members who thought that the program was elitist, creating a category of privileged faculty outside the traditional categories.

My view is very different. The appointment of university and distinguished faculty members who were both outstanding scholars and committed to our vision to be one of the foremost Christian research universities in America was and continues to be of enormous importance. For example, more than ever before Baylor's faculty was being noted in national publications whose audience was religious in outlook, such as *Christianity Today,* *Christian Century,* and *First Things.* This visibility included publications by our faculty and citations of the work of our faculty. I can recall on many occasions receiving these publications in the mail and discovering several Baylor faculty members in print in a single issue. To me this meant that Baylor was being recognized as never before in precisely the way our vision called for.

Simultaneous to this uptick in intellectual visibility was the enormous enhancement of the Baylor University Press. Under the able leadership of Carey Newman, the BUP went from publishing three or four books per year in the mid-1990s—almost always on parochial subjects—to publishing in the range of twenty-five books per year by 2005 on subjects of wide intellectual and academic interest. The authors included both Baylor scholars and scholars from across the United States.

Another direct outcome of the university and distinguished professors initiative was the creation of a few new PhD programs, the most important of which was philosophy. Along with Bill Cooper and Mike Beaty, I had encouraged the development of a PhD in philosophy in the mid-1990s, but the department—for good reasons—was not in a position to proceed with such an undertaking. Although the department was strong, there simply were not enough faculty members to make it work and the department did not have the financial backing to support the program at the level desired. But with the addition of Carl Vaught, Steve Evans, and Bob Roberts, and additional faculty such as Bob Kruschwitz, Doug Henry, and Todd Buras, the department was ready to move forward with a PhD program in 2003. Today the doctorate in philosophy, along with those in religion and literature, is one of the bellwether PhD humanities programs at Baylor. This is as it should be, given Baylor's vision to be the premier Christian university in the country.

# 11

# BAYLOR AT A CROSSROADS

---

The opening of the fall semester each year at Baylor was the occasion of a university-wide faculty meeting. While these were not pompous events akin to a commencement ceremony, they were rather grandiose and well attended. The standard agenda included the introduction—by the respective deans—of all new faculty members, school by school; a report on enrollment; a report on university finances; a speech from the provost; and a speech from the president. For the fall faculty meeting of 2000, held on August 17, the title of my talk was "Baylor at a Crossroads."

I described the crossroads before us as a university in straightforward language: "We can either maintain our present course, with appropriate fine-tuning along the way, or we can aspire to much higher levels of accomplishment and thereby become an academically and intellectually powerful university, indeed, one of the top two or three Christian universities in the world." I contended that if we chose the latter course, we would "raise our level of influence exponentially."

The faculty understood what I meant by "our present course." Traditionally Baylor had been a provider of undergraduate and professional education, and several of our programs had national reputations for excellence. I listed pre-med, law, certain fields of the humanities and social sciences, certain areas of the sciences, engineering and computer science, entrepreneurship and accounting, music and the arts, nursing, and international education. Moreover, as judged by the *U.S. News* annual survey of national undergraduate universities, we had been ranked for years on a regular basis in the second tier, around 75th in the country, putting us behind only the University of Texas among the Big XII schools at that time. It was not a bad place to be at all, and we should be proud of these accomplishments, I implied, but we were equipped to achieve more.

Our positive image in the world of higher education was based almost solely on the accomplishments of our graduates: governors, jurists, physicians, ministers, lawyers, public servants and politicians, educators, artists, business leaders, and the like. Because of our commitment to undergraduate education and to teaching, very little of our reputation as a university was based on Baylor's greatness as a center of intellectual leadership, whether in doctoral work, research and publications, grantsmanship, or our active participation in national conversations within the academy and in the wider culture, including in the church. There were, I said to the faculty, important exceptions to this claim in certain areas, but overall we were essentially an undergraduate university with a first-rate law school. To put the matter another way, the faculty at Baylor made its contribution to the common good largely through its teaching, not its scholarship independent of teaching.

This was confirmed, I maintained, by the just-released Carnegie classification of the comprehensive universities in which Baylor was then grouped within Texas: Texas A&M Commerce, Texas A&M Kingsville, Texas Southern, Texas Woman's University, University of Texas at Dallas, and University of Texas at El Paso. Baylor was not in the same category as Rice, SMU, University of Texas at Austin, Texas A&M, and Texas Tech, those institutions we considered our peers. While the Carnegie classification is not about rankings or quality, it did provide a perspective on our position in the academic world.

The position I took in the speech to the faculty was that while we should continue the tradition of great teaching at Baylor and be proud of it, we should build a university on that strong foundation, a Christian university, committed to being a center of intellectual influence. In order for this to occur, three goals needed to be achieved. First, we needed to invest in our faculty in an unprecedented way, including the recruitment of renowned scholars, especially Christian scholars, and top junior faculty. Second, we must develop a select number of top-flight academic programs. These would include, I said, not only undergraduate and professional programs, but also doctoral programs, research centers and institutes, an honors college, and a flourishing international education program. Third, we needed to recruit better students at both the undergraduate and graduate levels, but especially at the graduate level, including a focused program to recruit postdoctoral scholars within our PhD programs. I pointed out that if we could achieve these goals, Baylor would become a "powerful university academically and intellectually."

I suggested four strategies for the realization of these goals. The first was the casting of a comprehensive vision. In point of fact, that was already being done in nascent form as seen in statements from President Sloan and in various comments I had made publicly, including the notion that Baylor be one of the top-ranked Christian universities in the country.

The second strategy—not really a strategy perhaps, but that's what I called it—was generating the necessary will to move boldly toward the vision before us. This would be a huge challenge, I noted, because "some members of the larger Baylor community do not want their *alma mater* to change; they want Baylor to remain essentially a first-rate undergraduate school with focused strength in some professional areas."

The third strategy called for the creation of a plan that would enable us to identify substantive areas of excellence in our academic program overall. I went on to say, however, that whatever specific details emerge in our plan, "our efforts must be collaborative. . . . As we plan together, the administration commits itself to work with you in an open fashion, eager to hear your suggestions as we jointly press forward to achieve our higher goals."

And, fourth, we will need to raise sufficient resources to do the work we envision. For the next five years, I said, "perhaps the greatest priority of the University is to raise the money needed to support our academic mission at an unprecedented level. We hope that . . . the next major money-raising effort will be devoted entirely to the support of our academic programs alone." This would include funding for endowed chairs and professorships, program excellence, faculty development, and student scholarships.

I concluded my address by returning to a theme I introduced to the Board of Regents during my July 1992 reflections on Baylor's future. Are there models in higher education that we might follow? I suggested again that we might consider Notre Dame, but on this occasion I backtracked a bit. While we have learned much from them, their tradition and dominant constituency are different from ours. Baylor now stands alone in the world of Christian higher education. Then I spoke the following words:

To say much more than the obvious, Baylor's history and character are unique. We were born in 1845 out of the desire to promote learning "in all its branches" and to locate this learning within the context of the Gospel. Judge R. E. B. Baylor was an embodiment of this ideal, as was our first faculty member, who happened to be an Episcopalian. We were raised in controversy, as evidenced in the late nineteenth century, when an influential leader at the University of Texas tried to shut down Baylor because he believed we confused Christianity and higher education. In his view, schools such as Baylor should go out of existence.

But the men and women of Baylor have persisted in the conviction that no one else can do the work that we are called to do: to become a major intellectual center for academic study and research within the Christian tradition. Our intrinsic character and commitments are as strong as ever, and our national and international recognition is as strong as ever, in large part because of our very character and commitments. That is to say, Baylor has held firm to the conviction that there is no truth larger than God's truth, and thus that our own identity as a Christian university requires us to be academically fearless, rigorous, and bold.

I recall that when I finished my talk, Stan Madden, who had earlier in the faculty meeting given a report on enrollment, asked President Sloan within my hearing, "Did you know he was going to say that?" Sloan said "No," but he certainly knew my thinking on the subject of Baylor and the crossroads we faced.

# 12

# THE POLANYI AFFAIR

The lofty aspirations expressed in my crossroads speech to the faculty, along with the developments in graduate education, the new commitment to research, and the recruitment of renowned scholars, had taken a decidedly ugly turn in 1999–2000 with the establishment of the Polanyi Center. The center, named after the Hungarian scientist, Michael Polanyi, was created as a research unit to explore broadly the relationship between the sciences and religion, and in particular the then-recent developments appropriate to the claims of intelligent design.

The impetus for the founding of the Polanyi Center was the work of a brilliant young scholar, William Dembski, who held a PhD in mathematics and a PhD in philosophy, both from prestigious universities, and two masters degrees, one in statistics and one in theology. I had not heard of Dembski before 1999. He came to my attention by way of Mike Beaty, who was then director of our Institute for Faith and Learning, and who learned of Dembski from President Sloan.

I invited Dembski to Baylor for a visit with me on March 16, 1999, and we had a fascinating exchange. He told me about his personal history, which included a conversion to Christianity when he was about twenty years old. That experience propelled him to a life of purpose that he had not known before.

The central focus of our conversation was his interest in intelligent design, the general theory that the cosmos is too complex for its existence to have come into being simply by natural causes alone. In one way or another, the evolution of the natural world had to be guided, however discreetly, by some factor or agent outside itself. His illustration of this point was striking to me: Imagine that you throw a deck of playing cards out on the floor, he said, and by mere chance they fall into perfect order, from the two of clubs to the ace of spades. According to Dembski's explanation, the naturalist argues that the notion of chance and necessity would explain this phenomenon (see Jacques Monod, *Chance and Necessity*, 1970). That is, when applied to organisms, the only way the particular organism could exist at all is if it had within it the very properties, from the tiniest to the largest, to be what it is. This is the view of philosophical naturalism, that nature is self-contained. On the other hand, the non-naturalist would argue that the improbability of the cards falling into perfect order, or the organism to be what it is, is so extraordinarily high that some "intelligence" outside the event—cards or organisms—would be needed for it to occur as it does. The strict naturalist denies any place for such agency or causation.

Traditionally, Christians have held to the view that there are two "books" of revelation, Scripture and nature. They are mutually complementary and both are revelatory of one and the same God. According to Dembski, if the pure naturalists are right, there can be no complementarity between Scripture and nature, no intersection of faith and science. The two spheres are totally and completely independent. There can be no such thing as the integration of faith and science, and when the two simply go their separate ways, this leads to an impoverished view of nature, Dembski believed.

The intellectual problems posed by naturalists and non-naturalists led me to pursue the possibility of creating an administrative unit within the Institute for Faith and Learning during the spring of 1999. It seemed to me and others, including President Sloan, that such a unit would fit well within our broader vision to make Baylor a true intellectual center for those issues of interest to the academy, the church, and our broader culture. So, in pursuit of this goal, we invited Dembski back to the Baylor campus on April 20, 1999, to give an academic presentation sponsored jointly by the provost's office and the Institute for Faith and Learning. The lecture was well attended, mostly by faculty members and students from the philosophy department. The discussion after the lecture was animated at times, but overall was friendly.

Over the course of the next few weeks, I personally discussed with a few faculty members, including some in the sciences, what their views would be if we established a center for the study of the relationship of faith and science. I received no serious reservations, although in hindsight, I should have discussed the idea more broadly with the science faculty. I had no idea, however, that resistance would reach the level it did. We moved forward with plans to create the center, and following the suggestion of Dembski, we called the unit the Polanyi Center, to be located administratively within the Institute for Faith and Learning. Bill Dembski was to be the director and Bruce Gordon the associate director. Because their appointments were as research faculty, their time with Baylor would be on a contractual basis, not on a traditional faculty track. They started their work at Baylor in the fall of 1999.

The first big project of the center was a grand conference on the subject of "The Nature of Nature," held on the Baylor campus, April 12–15, 2000. The conference program included scientists (including two Nobel Laureates), philosophers, historians, and theologians. Approximately thirty plenary and breakout sessions covered a wide range of topics: "An Evolutionary Argument Against Naturalism," "Naturalism Undefeated," "Science Without God: Natural Laws and Christian Beliefs," "Science and Theism: Conflict or Coherence?" and "The Place of Teleology in Nature." Scholars and lay people alike attended in large numbers from across the country. The conference was funded by a combination of grants from the Templeton Foundation and the Discovery Center, as well as registration fees. The conference also received a lot of media attention, from our student newspaper, *The Baylor Lariat*, to *The Waco Tribune-Herald*, *The Houston Chronicle*, and *The Chronicle of Higher Education*.

The pushback from the Baylor faculty was almost immediate. The conference was boycotted by most faculty members, especially the science faculty who objected on ideological grounds and on the grounds that the Polanyi Center had been instituted without their input. But they also objected because many science faculty members felt a sort of embarrassment about Baylor being associated with what one faculty member declared was "stealth creationism." Rightly or wrongly, many saw the intelligent design project as a mere upgrade of a literal interpretation of the first three chapters of Genesis and feared a backdoor re-entry of fundamentalism at Baylor.

Thus, within a week after the conference, the Faculty Senate voted 27–2 that the Polanyi Center should be abolished.

President Sloan spoke directly to the issues surrounding the Polanyi Center in his annual "State of the University" address on April 20, 2000. He began his remarks as follows: "The establishment of the Michael Polanyi Center at Baylor University has generated a great deal of campus discussion these past few weeks and also attracted statewide media coverage. In light of the attention this Center and its work have received and the Baylor Faculty Senate's . . . resolution calling on the administration to dissolve the . . . Center, I feel it is important for me to respond." And respond Sloan did. First, he took issue with the claim that the center was established without any faculty consultation and that academic process had been violated. Yes, he admitted, we as an administration probably could have done some things "to manage the process more effectively." Notwithstanding, he went on, "there is a legitimate place [throughout higher education], and here at Baylor as well, . . . for administrative initiative in academic matters." Sloan held up as an example the creation at Baylor of the Center for Jewish and American Studies, established about the same time as the Polanyi Center. This center was also put into place by the administration, following the same protocol as that of the Polanyi Center, including the appointment of a university professor, Marc Ellis. This supposedly controversial action proceeded with no faculty objection.

Process was not the real issue; it was not "the heart of the matter," as many held. "In my experience," Sloan said, "people often object to 'the way things were done' as a rhetorical substitute for what was done." The real objection, Sloan maintained, was a substantive one, and he was not going to countenance a form of censorship on the work of the center. He said, "I believe there are matters of intellectual and academic integrity at stake here. Drs. Dembski and Gordon, both highly capable scholars with the credentials to support the . . . study that the Center was established to pursue, should be allowed to do their work." We should not be afraid to ask difficult questions, even if they are politically incorrect. Then he added: "Indeed, I am proud of Baylor's willingness to ask questions which some are apparently afraid to entertain."

Sloan concluded his talk by emphasizing that the future of the center and its work would not be settled on political or emotional grounds. Because we as a university remain committed to the principle of peer review, he said, "there will be an evaluation committee/panel established of largely external membership to consider the academic and intellectual legitimacy, from both scientific and extra-scientific grounds, of the work of the Center." Sloan called on everyone to support this evaluation effort and let the yet-to-be-appointed committed do its work. He pledged himself to take the recommendations of the committee with "utmost seriousness."

It was my task as provost, with substantial assistance from Dean Wallace Daniel, to assemble this evaluation committee. Over the next two months he and I consulted with a wide range of scholars at Baylor and elsewhere to name a committee that would be highly respected not only by those on both sides of the debate at Baylor, but also by the higher education community. My first recruit was the chair of the committee, Bill Cooper, former dean of the College of Arts and Sciences and long-time and revered member of the Baylor faculty. The full membership of the committee was announced on June 23, 2000: Bill Cooper, chair; William Abraham, Albert Cook Outler Professor of Wesley Studies at Southern Methodist University's Perkins School of Theology; Scott K. Davis, vice president for research at GenomicFX in Austin and former assistant professor of animal science at Texas A&M; Judith Dilts, chair of the biology department at William Jewell College; Cutberto Garza, professor of nutritional science at Cornell University; Elaine Lambert, clinical associate professor of medicine in rheumatology at Stanford University; Ernan McMullin, The John Cardinal O'Hara Professor Emeritus of Philosophy at the University of Notre Dame; John A. Moore, professor emeritus of biology at the University of California at Riverside; and Ronald Numbers, chair and professor in history of medicine at the University of Wisconsin. The committee was charged with assessing the purposes and activities of the Polanyi Center, assessing the effectiveness and appropriateness of the center's work, and providing recommendations about the center's future.

The committee convened on campus September 8–9, 2000. Each member had received in advance a large package of materials that included books and articles relevant to the evaluation. In addition to reviewing this material, the committee interviewed those persons from Baylor who had a direct interest in the committee's charge.

The final report of the committee, submitted to me and the Baylor administration on October 16, 2000, calls attention to Baylor's long and distinguished tradition in the sciences, one that is respected throughout the scientific community. The report also notes the natural interest at Baylor in the relationship of science and religion. "The university should continue to foster a broad range of scholarship in this domain and in this way contribute to the active dialogue between science and religion now in progress." The report adds that this dialogue should be dealt with "openly and freely" and would best be promoted under the broad umbrella of the Institute for Faith and Learning.

The report contained four specific recommendations for the university as it proceeds forward in the discussion of faith and science:

1. It is important for a university in the Christian tradition to take an active interest in issues involving the complex and changing relationships between science and religion. This mission can best be fostered by the University's Institute for Faith and Learning where it seems to be naturally at home. In pursuing this mission, room should be made for a variety of approaches and topics. It would clearly be too restrictive on the part of the Institute to focus attention in this area on a single theme only, such as the design inference.

2. Nevertheless, the Committee wishes to make it clear that it considers research on the logical structure of mathematical arguments for intelligent design to have a legitimate claim to a place in current discussions of the relations of religion and the sciences. Although this work, involving as it does technical issues in the theory of probability, is relatively recent in origin and has thus only just begun to receive response in professional journals, . . . the Institute should be free, if it chooses, to include in its coverage this line of work, when carried out professionally.

3. An advisory committee to the Institute for Faith and Learning, composed of Baylor faculty members, should be appointed to assist in planning and reviewing the science and religion component of the Institute.

4. [T]he Committee believes that the linking of the name of Michael Polanyi to programs relating to intelligent design is, on the whole, inappropriate. Further, the Polanyi name has come by now in the Baylor context to take on associations that lead to unnecessary confusion.

The committee concluded its report by acknowledging again the importance of the dialogue between science and religion, and with it "the flourishing of academic freedom."

I called a meeting of Bill Cooper, Mike Beaty, Bill Dembski, and Bruce Gordon on October 17 to discuss the final report of the committee.

Basically, the purpose of the meeting was for me to read the report in their presence. Initially Dembski seemed to be displeased with the report, but his attitude changed before we departed. I made it clear during the meeting that none of us in the room was to make any public comments about the report. All public comments would be left to President Sloan. In the public release of the report, Sloan stated: "I accept all of the committee's recommendations and have asked Provost Donald Schmeltekopf to implement them fully and specifically as soon as possible."

Before the day was done, however, Dembski issued his own press release in clear violation of my expressed instructions. His statement read as follows:

> The report [of the committee] marks the triumph of intelligent design as a legitimate form of academic inquiry. This is a great day for academic freedom. I'm deeply grateful to President Sloan and Baylor University for making this possible, as well as to the peer review committee for its unqualified affirmation of my own work on intelligent design. . . . My work on intelligent design will continue unabated. Dogmatic opponents of design who demanded the Center be shut down have met their Waterloo. Baylor University is to be commended for remaining strong in the face of intolerant assaults on freedom of thought and expression.

Naturally, we in the administration were greatly distressed by the content of this statement, given that it misrepresents the work of the review committee. We asked him to rescind his release, but he refused to do so. Therefore, on October 19, Dembski was relieved of his duties as director of the Polanyi Center. "The theme of the report emphasized the need for the individuals associated with the center to work in a collegial manner with other members of the Baylor faculty," stated Mike Beaty, who had general supervision over the center as director of the Institute for Faith and Learning. "Dr. Dembski's actions after the release of the report compromised his ability to serve as director." Bruce Gordon, associate director of the center, was named interim director. Dembski remained at Baylor as a research professor.

In consultation with Wallace Daniel, dean of the College of Arts and Sciences, we soon named an advisory committee to the Institute for Faith and Learning to review the science and religion component of the Institute's work, as recommended by the evaluation committee. In addition, the Polanyi name was removed from the work of the center. Gordon continued with Baylor through the 2000-01 academic year, but was not issued a new contract, and as no new director was named, the center ceased to exist. Dembski's contract as a research professor was honored to its completion in 2005.

## REFLECTIONS

The controversy surrounding the Polanyi Center and its work came as a surprise to me. I had no idea the creation of a research unit to investigate the intersection of religion and science would prompt such hostile reactions. Perhaps I was simply naïve, given that I had no ideological investment in the project of intelligent design. I was certainly not a proponent of "creationism" in any strict sense, professionally or personally. To me, intelligent design seemed like an interesting idea that people in a serious Christian university could reasonably think about. Drawing on philosophy, I was well aware of the design argument for the existence of God, as well as the argument from first cause. I had taught both for years to undergraduates, not as fact, of course, but as theories that might explain why there is something rather than nothing. Additionally, as an orthodox Christian, I affirmed the doctrine of God as Creator. My convictions, then, fall in the broad category of "theistic evolution."

Even now I wonder why we at Baylor couldn't have a sustained discussion about these issues, why we were unable to build on the stimulating and provocative conference, "The Nature of Nature"? Yes, we certainly should have handled the establishment of the Polanyi Center with more input from faculty, especially science faculty members. Without question we needed to be more aware of the professional concerns of our science faculty. But as President Sloan remarked, the widespread objection to the center was not based on how it was done, but what was done. That is, there was fundamental opposition to a research unit dedicated to the proposition that philosophical naturalism, implicitly embraced by many scientists in the academy, is ultimately unsatisfactory, philosophically or theologically.

As the external evaluation committee recommended, I appointed, with the help of Dean Daniel, an internal advisory committee to give us guidance on how best to proceed in the Institute for Faith and Learning's work at the intersection of religion and science. The members of the committee were: Bill Cooper (philosophy) and Ben Pierce (biology), co-chairs; David Arnold (mathematics), William Brackney (religion), Melissa Essary (law), Barry Hankins (history), Keith Hartberg (biology), Truell Hyde (physics), Kevin Pinney (chemistry), David Rudd (psychology), and Tina Thurston (anthropology). The committee met over the course of the 2001-02 academic year and did valuable work. They interviewed a large number of faculty members, including many in the sciences. The committee's written reports find that "there is widespread interest among Baylor faculty on the relationship of science and faith. A number of faculty members from across the sciences and humanities are currently engaged in teaching and scholarship that fall at the interface of science and religion." The advisory group went on to say that this interest notwithstanding, there is "no current program or administrative structure [that] exists to facilitate and encourage interaction among these activities. Given these existing interests and strengths and Baylor's religious identity, the committee recommends that an interdisciplinary program in science and religion be developed at Baylor."

Unfortunately, even over a decade later, no such program exists. The good-faith efforts surrounding the entire Polanyi episode were, in the end, a futile venture.

# 13

## ABNER MCCALL'S ADVICE
Planning and Faculty Encouragement

---

Late in the spring semester of 1991, about a month before I became the chief academic officer on June 1, I contacted Abner McCall, president emeritus and chancellor of Baylor, and asked for a meeting with him. He gladly consented. We met for about two hours in what was called the "Faculty Kitchen," a private area in the Bill Daniel Student Center where faculty members gathered for lunches. My purpose in meeting with Judge McCall was to get his advice on what should be my top priorities as the new provost. He said two things without a moment's hesitation: planning and faculty encouragement.

I took his advice on both counts. The planning part started with the first deans' retreat I organized, held on August 7–8, 1991, at the Stagecoach Inn in Salado, Texas. We began our discussion at 2:00 p.m. the first day, and concluded with lunch the second day. Our spouses joined us late in the afternoon on the first day, at which time we played volleyball and took a dip in the nice swimming pool at the Stagecoach Inn. Although the venue for the deans' retreat changed after two years—we gathered at Spring Lake near Aquila, Texas, for the following ten years—the agenda was essentially always the same: We began with reports from each dean or, occasionally, a dialogue with President Sloan when he was in attendance, followed by discussion, and then we played. It was always volleyball, and the spouses joined in. The deans were required to play, while the spouses played on a voluntary basis. We always had fun together and, as a result, built strong relationships over the years.

The topic of great import for the first deans' retreat was my proposal to create an optional core curriculum (see chapter 2, "Early Initiatives"). I explained in general terms what I had in mind, and I also provided the names of those who would form the ad hoc faculty committee to formulate a plan, to recommend a final curriculum proposal. It was important at this point that all the deans understand that this new core curriculum would be "optional," that is, that the program would be limited in number of students (200 per year) and that each school would be given the choice whether or not to participate. There was broad support for my proposal, although there was some skepticism that the program would actually work in practice. In any case, the deans were generally on board, and the proposal was passed by all the schools by the end of the spring semester of 1993.

This discussion at the first deans' retreat was a model for the kind of planning I thought was necessary for the academic division as a whole. In addition to whatever concerns and considerations the individual deans had in mind, I always had some agenda that needed to be promoted with all the deans. During one retreat in August of 2000, I focused our discussion on fund-raising by inviting Edward Kvet, dean of the College of Music and Fine Arts at Loyola University, to join us and discuss the kind of opportunities that deans in particular can cultivate for the purpose of fund raising. Another example was a discussion of Robert Benne's book, *Quality with Soul: How Six Premier Colleges and Universities Keep Faith with Their Religious Traditions,* led by Ralph Wood, university professor of theology and literature at Baylor. My aim for this retreat was to stimulate among all the deans a sense of strengthened vision about what a serious Christian university looks like. Other retreat topics included standards for tenure, levels of compensation, and performance evaluation, all characteristic issues for universities, but I wanted to be sure to avoid a reactive approach and instead proceed proactively. Or, as Judge McCall advised, by planning.

These kinds of retreats—proactively planning and discussing important university concerns, followed by fellowship—became a favorite device for President Sloan as well from the very beginning of his presidency. In fact, over the eight years that I served with him, we probably averaged some sort of planning retreat about once a semester, and usually our spouses would join us. One interesting feature of Sloan's retreats was his practice of rotating the presider of the retreats from one member of the executive council to another, rather than presiding over the retreat himself. For example, I recall that one such retreat was led by Tom Stanton, the athletic director. He wasn't the least bit shy about asking the other members to discuss their plans for the next year. In fact, he began with me. His opening question to me was, "Don, what are your plans for the academic division this coming year?"

One particularly noteworthy planning retreat involved a special guest from Notre Dame: the former provost, Timothy O'Meara. The context for this retreat was our early planning for Baylor 2012, the ten-year vision that would be adopted by the Board of Regents on September 21, 2001. O'Meara was an ideal consultant for us, as Notre Dame had gone through a significant planning process in adopting its ten-year vision in 1990, called the "Colloquy for the Year 2000." O'Meara was provost at the time, so he had direct experience with the kind of planning we needed to undertake in preparation for Baylor 2012.

A third significant planning effort launched during my provostship was the "academic summits," remarkable two-day events held at the White Bluff Resort in Whitney, Texas, always during the latter part of June. These were large gatherings, somewhere in the neighborhood of 100 people: members of the central administration, including the president and all the vice presidents, the deans, all department chairs, heads of other administrative units, other leaders of the faculty, such as members of the Faculty Senate, and assorted guests. The purpose of these summits was to bring together all those in leadership positions at Baylor in order to address the big issues of higher education.

With the help of a planning committee, I organized the summits around the pressing issues of the day in higher education. The inaugural summit held in June 1997 was on "Trends and Challenges in Higher Education." Our invited speaker was Carol Schneider, president of the American Association of Colleges and Universities (AAC&U). My connection with AAC&U went back several years, in fact, to when the organization was called the Association of American Colleges. I had several interactions with its prior president, Mark Curtis, and knew that the association appealed to religious colleges and universities. And so did Carol Schneider: she was conversant with religious questions and the issues surrounding church-related higher education in America and perhaps, more important than anything else, she was a great advocate for the liberal arts. This was particularly important in an era when professional education was becoming ever more popular with students.

The second summit addressed the issue of student retention. Our guest speaker was John Gardner, a professor from the University of South Carolina-Columbia and founder of the acclaimed "Freshman-Year Experience" program. Nobody knew the world of student retention any better than John Gardner. I first heard him speak in 1985 at the annual meeting of the Southern Association of Colleges and Schools in Atlanta, and he addressed the issue of retention in ways I had never considered before. Our year-to-year undergraduate retention rate at Baylor in 1998 was approximately 85 percent, which meant that with our student population, we were losing hundreds of students every year. I knew Gardner could help us at Baylor, and help us he did. In President Sloan's concluding remarks to the gathered group that year, he spoke with a new-found passion about our retention issues and proceeded to name me the chair of a university-wide task force on improving our retention success. For the next year, I met regularly with about twenty-five faculty and staff members to monitor the current student retention situation and to address plans for improvement. Student retention at Baylor has been an ongoing emphasis ever since.

The third summit, "Teaching, Learning, and Technology," dealt with the issue of technology in the educational process. Although I was something of a Luddite in the realm of technology—in 1999 I was just beginning to be proficient with the computer—I knew that Baylor needed to be up to speed with educational technology. I recruited David Brown, provost emeritus of Wake Forest University, as our speaker. I had known David for years as an administrator, not as a guru in educational technology, and yet while provost at Wake Forest, David led in the transformation of the university to what was labeled at Wake Forest as a "ubiquitous computing environment." One aspect of this was the issuance of a laptop computer to every Wake Forest student. David also demonstrated to the Baylor community how technology can enrich the classroom experience. Discussion groups at the summit focused on various questions, such as how technology can enhance student learning and what Baylor can do broadly to better support the use of technology on campus. Again, I was named the chair of a faculty-staff steering committee to review the summit's recommendations and determine how they would be addressed.

The fourth summit addressed the issues of evaluation and assessment. Our speaker on this occasion was Frank Horton, president emeritus of the University of Toledo and current interim president of Southern Illinois University. Eighty-five senior administrators, staff, deans, department chairs, and others attended. Discussion groups focused on matters related to the evaluation of teaching; the evaluation of department chairs, deans, and other administrators; tenure review and post-tenure review; and academic program review.

The fifth and final summit, held June 25–26, 2001, dealt with the question of the "common core." This issue arose out of our growing interest, following the establishment of the successful Baylor Interdisciplinary Core program, in broadening a common core curriculum for more of our students. This interest moved in two directions: one was a minimal requirement for all undergraduate students, and the other was our interest in creating a great text major. The guest speaker was Jeffrey Wallin, president of the American Academy for Liberal Education and former officer with the National Endowment for the Humanities, where I served in the mid-1980s. Wallin spoke about the qualities of an educated person, or what every "thoughtful person" should know, and then the discussion groups focused on five areas: Western and Christian intellectual traditions, foreign language and other cultural traditions, the sciences and mathematics, the arts, and society and its institutions.

I returned to the theme of a common core in my annual address to the faculty in the fall of 2001. There I said: "I can think of no better way to place before our undergraduate students the . . . ideas of higher learning at a Christian university than through a program centered on great texts. And the reason is this: the master works of the past expose students . . . to the formative and enduring ideas surrounding God, nature, and human life." This came right out of John Henry Newman's work, *The Idea of a University* (1899). Then I added: "When read with care and sympathy, these texts enlarge and transform the mind, giving it the capacity for critical intelligence."

I was still following Abner McCall's advice: planning and faculty encouragement. In the spring of 2002, a great text major and minor were approved by the College of Arts and Sciences and in 2003 made a part of the new Honors College.

## THE HARVARD EVENT

A surprising turn of events took place in early 2001. Marc Ellis, our new University Professor of American and Jewish Studies, received an invitation from Harvey Cox of the Harvard Divinity School to visit Harvard and bring with him a handful of other Baylorites, including President Sloan. The purpose of the gathering was for the Baylor folks to get an up-to-date perspective on the Divinity School, in hopes of Harvard's recruiting more Baylor graduates, and in turn for the Harvardians to get a fresh view of Baylor. At the last minute, President Sloan had to bow out, so I was asked to attend in his place, which I did. The others from Baylor who were invited to attend, in addition to Ellis and me, were Ralph Wood, William Brackney, chair of the religion department, Derek Davis, director of the Institute for Church-State Studies, and five Baylor students.

The visit, which occurred on March 21–22, 2001, began with an evening dinner on campus at the official residence of Dean Bryan Hehir, a Roman Catholic. After the usual introductions and pleasantries—there were about forty people present, mostly Divinity School faculty members—and after a delicious dinner, I was asked to make some comments about what had been going on at Baylor for the last decade or so. Of course, I knew exactly where to start: with the charter change. The essence of the change was very simple, from a governing board appointed by the Baptist General Convention of Texas to one largely self-perpetuating. The board would still be Baptist, but it would no longer be vulnerable to the whims of the Southern Baptist fundamentalist movement.

Most critics of the change, I noted, believed that Baylor would soon turn the way of virtually all other major Protestant universities of the past, namely, to a wholly secular identity. But that had not and was not happening at Baylor. To the contrary, Baylor was becoming more robustly Christian since the charter change than at any other time since World War II. I gave as evidence our emphasis on faith and learning, our active participation in the national network of church-related colleges and universities, our elevated standards for faculty hiring, including both higher academic and religious qualifications, the fact that I (and even the president for a period) personally interviewed all faculty candidates, and the inauguration of the new university and distinguished professors program (noting the hiring of both Ralph Wood and Mark Ellis in this regard), with its emphasis on bringing to Baylor distinguished Christian (and Jewish) scholars.

I then distributed copies of Baylor's mission statement to everyone present. This mission statement had been adopted by the Board of Regents in 1994 when we were preparing for the standard ten-year accreditation review by the Southern Association of Colleges and Schools. The content of the statement was decidedly influenced by the faith and learning discussion groups I had instituted in 1991. The core of the mission statement is summarized in one sentence: "The mission of Baylor University is to educate men and women for worldwide leadership and service by integrating academic excellence and Christian commitment within a caring community." But then I went on to read selected passages of the full mission statement that would drive home the essential Christian character of the Baylor enterprise. Here are the key passages I read:

> Established to be a servant of the church and of society, Baylor seeks to fulfill its calling through excellence in teaching and research, in scholarship and publication, and in service to the community, both local and global. The vision of its founders and the ongoing commitment of generations of students and scholars are reflected in the motto inscribed on the Baylor seal: *Pro Ecclesia, Pro Texana*—For Church, For Texas.

> *Pro Ecclesia.* Baylor is founded on the belief that God's nature is made known through both revealed and discovered truth. . . . In its service to the church, Baylor's pursuit of knowledge is strengthened by the conviction that truth has its ultimate source in God and by a Baptist heritage that champions religious liberty and freedom of conscience. . . . Affirming the value of intellectually informed faith and religiously informed education, the University seeks to provide an environment that fosters spiritual maturity, strength of character and moral virtue.

> *Pro Texana.* Integral to its commitment to God and to the church is Baylor's commitment to society. Whereas that society in the mid-1800s was limited to Texas, today Baylor's sphere of influence is indeed the world. The University remains dedicated to the traditional responsibilities of higher education—dissemination of knowledge, transmission of culture, search for new knowledge, and application of knowledge. . . .

> *Pro Ecclesia, Pro Texana.* Baylor University is committed to excellence at the undergraduate, graduate and professional levels. . . . Baylor encourages all of its students to cultivate their capacity to think critically, to assess information from a Christian perspective,

to arrive at informed and reasoned conclusions, and to become lifelong learners. . . .

Advancing the frontiers of knowledge while cultivating a Christian world-view, Baylor holds fast to its original commitment—to build a university that is *Pro Ecclesia, Pro Texana.*

I was uncertain what kind of discussion might ensue when I finished my remarks. Would I be attacked by the Harvard folks for advocating what could be construed by some as a narrow and constricting vision for higher education? There were a couple of mild comments in that direction, but the Reverend Peter Gomes, the highly regarded Minister to the University and one of the most popular professors at Harvard, soon weighed in. Later Ralph Wood would summarize Gomes's response to my comments: "Gomes declared that he had heard our provost's presentation and read our Mission Statement with great admiration, envy, and caution." Gomes then proceeded to clarify and explain, Wood wrote: "*admiration* because he knows of no other major institution of higher learning which seeks to maintain such academic rigor and Christian identity at the same time, *envy* because he knows that Harvard could never do any such thing, and *caution* because, if we ever lose this clear mission and purpose, we will never get it back."

This cautionary note came out of direct experience for Gomes, who related with sadness the fate of his *alma mater*, Bates College of Maine. When he was a student there in the early 1960s, the college still had strong ties to its Baptist heritage, but now it is not remotely religious. This change, he said, led him to resign recently as a member of its governing board after serving twenty-two years. According to Wood's account, "Gomes noted that Bates's decline came from the decision to hire 'Harvard nerds,' as he called them, rather than teachers and scholars committed to promoting and preserving the Bates religious tradition." Gomes also lamented the uncertain direction of the Harvard Divinity School, along with the loss of any religious purpose of Harvard University itself.

The conversation continued. I recall later hearing from some present that they could not remember a dinner discussion at Harvard that embodied such frankness as what we experienced together. But there was one other important comment made, this from Richard Parker, a professor in the Kennedy School for Public Policy. Wood reports that "Parker teaches one of the most heavily subscribed graduate courses at Harvard: it deals with the real ways in which religious considerations continue to animate our public life, even if these concerns remain largely occluded from public view." At the Harvard dinner, Wood observed, "Parker declared that the intelligentsia and the journalists of America have not yet discovered this great salient fact—that evangelical Christianity is the most vigorous form of Protestantism left in the country. Vital Christianity and intellectual vigor are therefore located in schools like Baylor."

Our visit at Harvard continued the next day, under the warm hospitality of our host, Harvey Cox. We visited a couple of seminars, and Wood, Ellis, and Brackney had a formal dialogue with three Harvard faculty members about the nature of public theology in our time. One of the things we learned from our host was that the Divinity School had recently established a new chair in Evangelical Theology. This fact was no doubt involved in the invitation we received to visit Harvard and send more of our students their way.

Interestingly, the *Boston Globe* wrote a story about our visit while we were there, owing to the involvement of Harvey Cox. The story was in turn picked up by the AP wire service, catching the attention of both the Religious News Service and the *Dallas Morning News*. A *Dallas Morning News* reporter soon called me for an interview about our Harvard visit, producing yet another news story. The publicity continued for the next two months in various religious periodicals. The "Baylor-Harvard dialogue," as the event came to be known, had "legs," and some people even wondered when members of the Harvard faculty would visit Baylor. No such thing happened, of course. Trafficking with Harvard is only in one direction.

# 14

# BAYLOR 2012

---

By the year 2000, institutional planning had increasingly become part of the agenda at Baylor. President Sloan would wade into the matter from time to time in meetings of the executive council and with the regents. In fact, I think we had such discussions dating back to 1999, if not sooner. As I have already noted in chapter 11, "Baylor at a Crossroads," I spoke on the subject of institutional planning myself in my address to the faculty on August 17, 2000. The first sentence of my address was, "I believe Baylor is at a crossroads in its history." If we were going to aspire to higher levels of accomplishment than ever before, I contended, we needed to develop a strategy that encompassed four things, two of which were the development of a comprehensive vision and then a plan to match it.

The deans' retreat in August of 1999 was devoted to strategic planning. Stan Madden, vice president for university relations and professor of marketing in the Hankamer School of Business, met with us. At this time Stan was becoming active in our institutional commitment to strategic planning. Through the time together at the retreat, we collectively created our own version of a strategic planning process which we called the "SPP." Simply put, the SPP would entail goals, strategies, and action steps. This kind of thinking is often foreign to academics, but at the retreat, we all put our minds to the task. Each dean agreed to submit his or her plan to me in narrative form by April 2000 that would include the vision and goals of the dean's respective academic unit, how these goals were compatible with those of the university, and some estimate of the overall budget impact.

All of this was to be within the context of what President Sloan was urging the university community to do. Here is how he put it in his chapter in the book, *The Baylor Project: Taking Christian Higher Education to the Next Level* (2007):

> I challenged the university community to consider thought-fully essentially two questions: (1) based upon our history, who are we as an institution? and (2) what would we want Baylor to look like in the year 2012? It was an exercise in "visioning" that is very common on university campuses (as well as in for-profit and not-for-profit organizations all across the world). It was of course not intended to be a self-study. It was intended as an imaginative, envisioning experience which would challenge each of us and all of us to dream about what Baylor could truly become, if we were faithful to our historic identity as a Christian institution with a commitment to academic excellence and were willing to push ourselves over a ten-year period.

Although the strategic planning process got underway with the deans' retreat in August 1999, the "visioning" part began to take shape in the fall of 2000. Among other things, this meant clarifying what we mean when we speak of Baylor as a Christian university and what we mean when we speak of our commitment to academic excellence. For both we needed carefully considered ideas and language.

Who might provide such ideas and language? Coincidentally (or providentially, I would say), we had just recruited a new distinguished professor of ethics in the philosophy department, Bob Roberts. Bob came to us from Wheaton College, a school that understood well the meaning of a Christian institution of higher education. Moreover, as part of his Baylor contract, Bob was granted a sabbatical his very first year with us since he was scheduled to have a sabbatical year from Wheaton had he stayed there. Additionally, we agreed he could continue to live in the town of Wheaton for the year.

I asked Bob if he would help us on the visioning aspect of our plan, that is, write a draft of what such a vision might be and he readily agreed. Over the next few months Bob, from his home in Wheaton, wrote some of the essential parts of our grand vision. Here is a key passage in the final *Baylor 2012* document that marvelously expresses, from the pen of Bob Roberts, the essence of our vision:

It is a legacy of modernity to believe that the pathway divides between the uncompromising pursuit of intellectual excellence and intense faithfulness to the Christian tradition. Many universities and colleges, founded in the eighteenth or nineteenth century by devout men and women for the service of the church and the world in the name of Christ, later turned down the secular fork of this imaginary path. Indeed, this is the story of the greatest American universities: Harvard, Yale, Princeton, the University of Chicago. Accepting the same premise of the divided way, many Christian colleges have chosen insularity and self-protective intellectual mediocrity as the way to preserve their Christian vitality. But the idea that faith and learning are mutually exclusive has a weaker grip today than it had during most of the last century, and we at Baylor believe that that fork in the path is indeed a figment of the modern imagination. We believe that the highest intellectual excellence is fully compatible with orthodox Christian devotion. Indeed, the two are not only compatible, but mutually reinforcing. Christian faith, at its best, motivates a love of all truth; and true knowledge supports and deepens our love of God in Jesus Christ. This is, at any rate, the undivided way and ancient premise on which Baylor ventures into the next ten years of our exciting history.

To do well those things that are right suggests a course of action that is both excellent and faithful. "Excellence" is often a modern mantra divorced from ethical and moral content. We will seek, however, the achievement of worthy goals. It is precisely faithfulness to the spiritual and religious content of our Christian heritage which drives us to pursue excellence in all matters essential to our mission as both an academic community and as an institution of higher learning. This vision for 2012 can thus be presented and understood as a pursuit, with faithfulness to our heritage as expressed in our core convictions, of academic excellence and community excellence.

Thus, the pursuit of academic and community excellence, undergirded by our Christian heritage, was proclaimed as the vision of Baylor University.

*Baylor 2012* goes on to say that while each academic unit within Baylor has its own "issues, priorities, and constraints," they all share these six unifying themes grounded in particular beliefs.

Because we believe that all truth is open to human inquiry, Baylor University supports academic programs, within and across disciplines, which encourage the vigorous and open pursuit of truth by all the methods of scholarship.

Because we believe that human life has meaning and purpose, we support academic programs that seek to illuminate that meaning and purpose and to enrich human life through the creative and artistic works of intellect and imagination.

Because we believe that truth is open to inquiry and that human beings have obligations both to human communities and to nature, Baylor University supports academic programs and research that add to the sum of human knowledge and that apply knowledge to the technological, scientific, and cultural advancement of society.

Because we believe that human beings are part of nature yet have been given responsibility as stewards of it, Baylor University supports academic programs that investigate the natural world, increase understanding of the symbiotic relationship between human beings and the natural world, and protect the environment by encouraging good stewardship of natural resources.

Because we believe that we have responsibility to care for our health and well-being and that of others, Baylor University supports academic and extracurricular programs which seek to promote human physical, mental, and spiritual health.

Because we believe that individuals have moral and ethical obligations to communities, Baylor University supports academic programs that recognize the importance of human institutions, promote an understanding of and responsible participation in economic and social systems, foster citizenship, enhance community, and encourage service.

This is indeed visionary. Even now, it is hard for me to conceive of more appropriate ideas and language to express what Baylor can and should aspire to be. Yes, not everyone was inspired by these ideas. But one thing came across loud and clear once *Baylor 2012* was adopted and became widely accessible to the outside world: the sort of faculty members we were trying to recruit to Baylor were immensely impressed by our vision. In fact, we were told again and again in the interview process that *Baylor 2012* was the primary reason many faculty candidates were attracted to Baylor in the first place.

The vetting process for *Baylor 2012* took place during fall 2000 and spring 2001. It should be said that *Baylor 2012* began as an initiative of the administration. In that sense, it was a "top-down" development. However, there was wide input from across the campus in its content and actual writing, especially in the academic component, which represents well over half the document (excluding the concluding imperatives). One noteworthy section is about the faculty, in which the following, concluding sentence appears:

> To become a premier university, Baylor will need to compete for the most talented, energetic, and dedicated faculty—selected and retained not just on the basis of technical competence, scholarly power, and Christian belief, but also for Christian personal qualities such as integrity, humility, courage, community-mindedness, empathy, and wisdom, and for the variety of skills necessary to mentor students.

In other words, Baylor was looking for faculty members who combined in themselves intellect, faith, and virtue.

The academic part of *Baylor 2012* is comprised of four sections: undergraduate studies, graduate studies and research, professional studies, and research centers and institutes. Two emphases of the undergraduate studies part are the core curriculum (the "arts of human inquiry") and the honors college. Regarding the latter, the document states that we "will create an Honors College as a new administrative unit which will hire and tenure some of its own faculty and will coordinate the Honors Program, the University Scholars Program, the Baylor Interdisciplinary Core and a new Great Texts Program." The graduate studies and research section focused on "interdisciplinary niches" that would take advantage of some of our natural strengths, such as theology, philosophy, and literature. The pursuit of interdisciplinary work was also promoted for the areas of the health sciences and the environment.

The section on professional studies points out the importance of the core curriculum for all its majors. In addition, the document states that all the professional programs—business, education, engineering and computer science, music, nursing, law, and the seminary—should be "fundamentally informed and guided by the six primary themes which mark the Baylor academic community." The final section focuses on research centers and institutes. Here the theme of interdisciplinary work is emphasized again, including with graduate teaching, basic and applied research, publication programs, and service on behalf of a wide variety of constituents inside and outside the university. The vision expressed in the academic part of *Baylor 2012* also acknowledges the importance of an outstanding library system that provides access to a full range of intellectual resources.

What it means to be a community of excellence is articulated in the next ten pages of the document. Sweeping ideas are expressed in this part of *Baylor 2012*. For example: "The soul of Baylor rests in its ability to impact the quality of the human condition by graduating individuals who reflect the character of the Christian faith." Another: "Baylor will serve as a training ground for the development of healthy relationships across racial, ethnic, and gender lines, thus providing the country with a new generation of individuals committed to faith, service and community." And this: "The concept of 'place' is indispensable in the building of true community. . . . The Baylor experience is centered in a physical campus, a geographical location in which students, faculty and staff gather to discover and express their sense of divine calling."

These were the ideas being vetted by the faculty and staff during fall 2000 and spring 2001. Different venues were employed, but of particular importance was the wide electronic distribution of complete drafts of the document, once in late 2000 and another in early 2001. Departments and schools were invited to respond in the first case, and single individuals were invited to do so in the second. Since I personally coordinated these efforts with the faculty, I can attest to the fact that most of the suggestions communicated to me were incorporated into the published document.

The final part of *Baylor 2012*—"imperatives for excellence"—was in effect an action plan. This was a consolidated effort by the administration to lay out the road ahead, but there is no doubt that this section was primarily the work of Robert Sloan. Here is how the document reads: "We now draw from the foregoing vision of Baylor in 2012 a set of 12 imperatives that reflect our core convictions and are designed to push the University to a level of excellence that will propel us into the ranks of the nation's Tier One colleges and universities." I will simply list the imperatives without discussion:

I. Establish an environment where learning can flourish.

II. Create a truly residential campus.

III. Develop a world-class faculty.

IV. Attract and support a top-tier student body.

V. Initiate outstanding new academic programs in selected areas.

VI. Guide all Baylor students, through academic and student life programming, to understand life as a stewardship and work as a vocation.

VII. Provide outstanding academic facilities.

VIII. Construct useful and aesthetically pleasing physical spaces.

IX. Enhance involvement of the entire Baylor family.

X. Build with integrity a winning athletic tradition in all sports.

XI. Emphasize a global education.

XII. Achieve a two-billion dollar endowment.

On at least two occasions, the draft of the vision and planning docu-ment was taken to the Board of Regents for discussion and comment. On both occasions the members of the board participated actively in assessing the document and making suggestions. Discussions surrounding the fund-ing of the plan were of special interest, and here the work of David Brooks was critical. At the time Brooks was the chief financial officer of the uni-versity. Regarding Brooks's efforts, Sloan wrote the following in *The Baylor Project*: "The ten-year vision would not have happened without the genius of David Brooks and all those who supported him in the development of its financial model."

On September 21, 2001, the Baylor University Board of Regents unan-imously approved the Baylor 2012 vision. Baylor had taken a historic turn in its quest to be a world-class Christian university.

## GRADING BAYLOR 2012

Five years after the adoption of *Baylor 2012*, I was invited as provost emeri-tus to speak before the Friends of Baylor to give my assessment on "how we were doing at mid-point." Comprised of regents, alumni, and other in-fluential Baylor supporters from across Texas, the Friends of Baylor was an organization formed in 2003 to lend support—political and financial—to the cause of advancing Baylor's Christian mission and to Robert Sloan's presidency. The gathering was held on October 21, 2006, at a downtown office building in Waco. Dary Stone, a member of the Board of Regents, presided at the meeting.

My approach to the question was simple: I gave a letter grade to each imperative as a means of assessing where we were on each. The grades ranged from A+ for academic facilities to D+ for endowment, with an overall grade of B for all twelve imperatives. My focus in the talk, however, was on developing a world-class faculty and on initiating outstanding new academic programs. With respect to developing a world-class faculty, I gave us a B. *Baylor 2012* states: "Baylor will recruit faculty from a variety of backgrounds capable of achieving the best of scholarship, both in teaching and research. We will recruit high-potential junior faculty and highly esteemed senior faculty who embrace the Christian faith."

There can be no doubt that we had made tremendous strides over the past several years in hiring just the kind of faculty our vision calls for, I said. How have we done this? By having the proper hiring guidelines in place, by urging all departments to take Baylor's total mission seriously in the hiring process, and by having senior administrators who are willing to say "no" to some recommendations that come forward from departments when it is clear the recommended candidate does not fit Baylor's mission. I said directly: "The bottom line is that every permanent faculty hire needs to meet a very certain test: Is he or she a Baylor 2012 kind of faculty member?" I then went on to mention a couple of worries, an explanation of why I gave us a B rather than an A. The first was that I saw evidence that some want to back off this test and move to a standard of professional competence only. The second was a growing reluctance to hire outstanding senior faculty members, such as distinguished professors, who are also Christian scholars in their own right. The regents, I said, must hold administrators accountable for Baylor 2012 kind of faculty hiring.

Additionally, as important as faculty hiring is, I said, we must also give attention to faculty development. I used an analogy here from football. A good football coach must not only recruit good players, but also coach them in fundamentals and how to execute the particular offense of the team. I then said this: "Most faculty members we recruit to Baylor do not come ready made to run our special 'offense,' which is that of a Christian research university. They have their disciplinary fundamentals in place, and we hope all of them are committed Christians, but many will be clueless about what a Christian university really is." So, I pointed out, we have to coach them and here, too, I had a worry. Our four-day orientation program for new faculty had now been reduced to a day-and-a-half. Further, new faculty had been told—perhaps a false rumor—that two-to-three hours per week of research would be enough to succeed at Baylor, where in reality it should be closer to that many hours per day. Hence, for both hiring and development, I gave imperative three a grade of B.

With respect to initiating new academic programs, *Baylor 2012* states: "We will continue our strong tradition of undergraduate and professional education, but greatly increase our scholarly output and our influence on society and the intellectual world by developing new doctoral programs, institutes, and centers, while enhancing existing ones." Here I gave us a grade of A- and suggested: "Perhaps this is the area in which the most positive developments have occurred since the inception of 2012." I gave as one example the Honors College, noting both its outstanding academic programs and its living and learning arrangements in Alexander and Memorial halls. Even more impressive are new PhD programs in mathematics, philosophy, political science, and exercise, nutrition, and preventive health, as well as a new doctoral track in sociology of religion.

However, one of the most exciting developments in our academic program, I noted, was the Institute for Studies of Religion (ISR). Never before in the history of Baylor has a research entity received such notice and acclaim as was recently the case with the ISR's report on "Religion in America," a national survey of religious values, practices, and behaviors. This is a great example, I said, of the institutional embodiment of one part of *Baylor 2012*. What happened here was not a fluke. "This research institute," I said, "was designed to do just this kind of work. . . . In fact, in a meeting recently with the director of the institute, Byron Johnson, he stated the case succinctly: 'This project is all about 2012.'"

I ended my talk of October 2006 on a somber note. "For some time now there has been a power struggle going on at Baylor, one having much to do with *Baylor 2012*. There are a considerable number of Baylor folks . . . who seem not to want *Baylor 2012* to succeed, in spite of the fact that few say so publicly." And then I continued: "This ongoing situation has now come to produce two cultures at Baylor, one I will call a 'Baylor 2012 culture,' and the other simply a 'resistance culture.' The resistance culture exists at one of two levels—the academic and/or the religious." Whatever the level, what is now required, I argued, is strong leadership, leadership from the regents, the president, the provost, deans, department chairs, and the like. The status quo will not be acceptable if our *Baylor 2012* plan is to have long-term success.

# 15

# SIGNIFICANT CHANGES IN THE PROVOST'S OFFICE

---

Several major administrative changes in the provost's office were made over the summer of 2001. Thomas Charlton, professor of history and vice provost for research, was appointed to a new position, vice provost for administration. Truell Hyde, associate professor of physics and director of the Center for Astrophysics, Space Physics and Engineering Research, was named the new vice provost for research. And David Jeffrey, distinguished professor of literature and humanities, was named to a new position, senior vice provost.

In 1992, during my second year as chief academic officer, I invited Tom Charlton into my administration as assistant vice president for academic affairs. Tom, a Baylor graduate who received his PhD in history from the University of Texas-Austin, joined the Baylor faculty in 1970. He knew everybody, a fact that would prove helpful to me, and he was a man of wonderful demeanor. We were loyal associates for eleven years.

I asked Dianna Vitanza to join my administration as vice provost for academic affairs in 1995. Also a Baylor graduate, Dianna became a member of the English department in 1982 and during the 1992-93 academic year, served as chair of the Faculty Senate. Dianna and I worked together extensively that year on the issue of merit pay. President Reynolds had indicated to me that merit pay should be instituted for the Baylor faculty and I promoted the idea with the Deans' Council, on which Dianna served as chair of the Senate. She supported the idea and she and I jointly hammered out the details of a policy statement on merit pay, even though she participated in the face of serious opposition from some faculty members. I was so impressed with Dianna's clear thinking on the subject that I invited her to be a part of the academic administration. She too was an important colleague in the provost's office for many years.

Though one of Dianna's most important contributions was as founding editor of Baylor's faculty handbook, first published in 1997, two of her other contributions should be noted, both having to do with new faculty members. One of these was the creation of a seminar for new faculty members, called "Scholarship and the Christian University," coordinated and led by Dianna and Mike Beaty, director of the Institute for Faith and Learning and associate professor of philosophy. The first of these seminars was held in August of 1998 and then annually with the purpose of introducing new faculty members to the mission and culture of Baylor, helping them to reflect in particular on the ways their faith and their academic discipline intersect. Dianna's other contribution was the initiation, in the academic year 1999-2000, of a mentoring program for new faculty members. Each new tenure-track assistant professor was paired with a Baylor senior professor who would in turn act as a resource for all the issues and challenges one might face as a new faculty member. This guidance was designed to help the new faculty member professionally and with respect to his or her social integration into the campus.

Tom Charlton, Dianna Vitanza, and I worked together as an administrative team for several years. However, by spring 2001, it became increasingly apparent to me that we needed to increase the funded research efforts of our faculty, especially of the science and engineering faculty members. Therefore, I asked Truell Hyde to assume the duties of the vice provost for research. As a research scientist, Truell had considerable experience in the area of sponsored research working with various public and private agencies. He knew what had to be done in the pursuit of grants and he was a great encourager of others to do the same.

Sponsored research had never been a priority at Baylor primarily because of the dominance of the teaching function of the faculty. Interestingly, the evolution of sponsored research illustrates the dramatic shift that had taken place at Baylor beginning in the late 1990s and extending into the 2000s. For example, in 1995 the total amount of sponsored-program expenditures was approximately 2.5 million. In 2001 the amount was about 6.5 million. In 2005 it was approximately 11.5 million. In 2014 sponsored-program expenditures reached to 27 million. This puts Baylor solidly in the Carnegie classification of "high research activity," where we were classified in 2006. Truell Hyde continues to serve effectively as vice provost for research.

When Tom Charlton assumed the new position of vice provost for administration in 2001, he immediately took on a huge assignment—preparing a proposal to house the George W. Bush Presidential Library at Baylor. In fact, Tom had already begun some background work on the project even before Mr. Bush was elected president, and Tom was well suited for the job. He knew Texas politics and he knew something about presidential libraries, given his connections with the Lyndon Baines Johnson Library at the University of Texas. After President Bush began serving in January 2001, Tom was full-steam ahead. He explored the makings of a proposal with associates not only at UT-Austin, but from other presidential library sites as well. He made visits to Washington, DC, to learn more about what was involved in the selection process, including the federal laws and regulations governing presidential libraries. In addition, he travelled across much of Texas giving talks about Baylor's interest in securing the George W. Bush Library. Eventually, Tom's efforts on behalf of the library project were passed on to Tommye Lou Davis in President Sloan's office. A heroic effort was made to get the library, but in the end, it was not to be. As matters played out, the planned site for the presidential library ended up being the ideal location for a beautiful new football stadium—McLane Stadium—on the Brazos River.

Tom Charlton was also involved in the formulation of the proposal for the Honors College, which was his last major project in the provost's office. We had been thinking about launching an honors college for some time. In fact, it was one of the recommendations contained in *Baylor 2012*. As the name suggests, the Honors College was designed to challenge the most academically gifted students who would come to Baylor. The college would be a new administrative unit of the university, having its own dean, faculty, and programs. Of the college's four central programs—the honors program, the university scholars program, the Baylor Interdisciplinary Core, and the great texts program—only the great texts program was new.

The others had a history at Baylor, but were not organizationally connected. Now they would be.

Based on the proposal Tom had written, we presented the operational concept of this new academic unit to the Board of Regents at its regular meeting on February 22, 2002. It was approved, and soon we began recruiting new faculty members to serve in the college. One of these new faculty hires was the inaugural dean, Thomas Hibbs, who was also named distinguished professor of ethics and culture. He began his work at Baylor effective July 1, 2003. Today the Honors College stands as one of the most important and prestigious academic units of the university.

Dianna Vitanza stepped down from her position as vice provost for academic affairs in June 2002. Mike Beaty replaced her, but with the title vice provost for faculty development. Mike continued all the initiatives in the area of faculty development, with emphasis on new faculty members. But a major new initiative was also launched: vocation for a liberal arts education. This project was funded by a Lilly Network Mentoring grant and a two million dollar grant from the Lilly Foundation, called Baylor Horizons. This new initiative was comprised of various components over several years, but the start-up activity was a series of faculty retreats on the theme of "Vocation, Liberal Learning, and the Professions." The first of these occurred on May 19–23, 2003, at Laity Lodge in the Texas hill country and involved approximately fifty faculty members.

The most significant new appointment in the provost's office in 2001 was appointing David Jeffrey, who had joined our faculty as distinguished professor of literature and humanities in 2000, to the role of senior vice provost. David came to us from the University of Ottawa where he had served for a number of years, including a term as chair of the English department. Even prior to his role in the provost's office, David was enormously helpful to us in the administration by identifying prospective new faculty members, including senior faculty who would embrace our distinctive Christian mission. Thus, in May 2001, we created the new position, senior vice provost, with the primary task of recruiting, mentoring, and retaining new faculty members.

David took an active role in the search for new faculty members, including especially distinguished scholar-teachers. He also helped organize new faculty development opportunities that focused on faith-related subjects, such as "Classic Arguments for the Existence of God: Augustine, Anselm and Aquinas," led by Carl Vaught, our distinguished professor of philosophy. But David's most important responsibility was recruiting new faculty members. He participated with me and others in the interviewing of virtually every candidate for open faculty positions, and for the academic year 2001-02, we interviewed close to two hundred faculty candidates. During this particular time period at Baylor, we were expanding our faculty as never before with lecturers, regular faculty members, and university and distinguished professors. We recruited three in the latter category alone.

An important development at this time was the creation of the Center for Religious Inquiry Across the Disciplines (CRIAD). The purpose of CRIAD was to engage in interdisciplinary research surrounding questions of religion. David served as chair of the planning committee of CRIAD and indeed was the ideal choice to undertake this assignment and to begin the process of bringing the project to fulfillment. Today this center—known now as the Institute for Studies of Religion—is perhaps the centerpiece of Baylor's public identity as a serious Christian research university.

## REFLECTIONS

During the twelve years I served as provost at Baylor, I had high regard for everyone who was a part of the provost's office—administrators and staff alike—and indeed continue to have personal relationships with all of them. I have been in their homes and they have been in mine, and I know their spouses and they all know and appreciate my wife, Judy. In fact, for over ten years a group of us—we dubbed ourselves the "Dearly Beloved"—have continued to get together from time to time, to break bread and to celebrate birthdays. One of our favorite times is always at Christmas when we gather at my home to share a meal and to exchange gifts.

Cynthia Dougherty, who worked with my predecessor, John Belew, was with me at the beginning as the assistant dean for academic services, which means she had the important task of managing all academic personnel records, including faculty status and all faculty contracts. Cynthia was succeeded in 1999 by Lois Ferguson, who joined us from the deans' office of the College of Arts and Sciences. My first assistant was Beverly Locklin who came to the provost's office from the philosophy department. She was succeeded in 1996 by Paulette Edwards, who came to the office from the sociology department. Paulette's title was assistant to the provost. Paulette was exceptionally gifted in managing the details of office work—and, importantly, my daily schedule. In fact, I have relied on my pocket calendars, which she prepared, and her own records to recall much of what these memoirs entail.

With a reliable staff keeping the office running smoothly, Tom Charlton, Dianna Vitanza, and I formed a close-knit team of administrators who worked together successfully for several years. The office environment, however, did change somewhat when David Jeffrey joined us in 2001. David is not only a dominant figure physically at six feet, five inches in height, he is also a forceful personality and one of the most learned individuals I have ever known. One bit of evidence of this learning is David's command of several languages. It was not unusual at all for David to revert momentarily to a second language during the course of a faculty interview. I never thought he was trying to impress anybody; it was just David being himself.

Within a year, by May 2002, however, it was becoming increasingly clear to me that other significant changes were in the offing. That will be the story of the next chapter.

# 16

# TAKING STOCK AND
# THE NEXT TRANSITION

---

I served as provost through May 2003. By the fall of 2001, however, President Sloan and I were already talking about how to have a smooth transition from my service as provost and to that of my successor. These conversations were totally confidential. Thus, everyone was surprised when I announced my retirement as provost in my address to the faculty on August 22, 2002. I opened my talk, "Taking Stock," with these words:

> From time to time in the life of an institution it is important to take stock of where we are and of what has been achieved in a given era, and today is such a time. In my remarks for this university faculty meeting, I want to reflect back on the last twelve years, the decade of the 1990s to the present, offering some historical perspective on the academic life of Baylor and pointing to some important issues to be faced this year and in the years ahead.

I devoted the first part of my talk to recounting some of the major events in Baylor's recent history, the most important of which was the charter change (see chapter 1). The reactions to that change, I said, were cast along a wide political spectrum. There was a lament from the right that Baylor would inevitably slide into "the iron grip of secularism," following the path of many other once-religiously affiliated colleges and universities over the past century or so in the United States; a celebration from the left that Baylor was now free from the "religious shackles" that had long prevented it from becoming a prestigious modern university; and, thirdly, a growing realization from the moderate center that Baylor could now pursue its own course as a serious Christian university, a university "both intellectually enlightened and religiously faithful," indeed, "a university that could provide the kind of leadership in the Protestant and free-church tradition that Notre Dame represented within the Roman Catholic community." The Baylor board and administration were committed to the third view, and it was with these goals in mind that I served as chief academic officer of Baylor since June 1991.

I enumerated the significant accomplishments over the past decade or so, and the list was lengthy: the creation of the Baylor Interdisciplinary Core; a merit-pay system; new faculty development opportunities; the growth of international education, spurred by the newly endowed Jo Murphy Chair in International Education; the creation of three new schools, engineering and computer science, Truett seminary, and social work; the establishment of five new PhD programs: biology, sociology of religion, church-state studies, mathematics, and philosophy; the enhancement of information technology; the founding of the Baylor Symposium; the expansion of the core curriculum required of all students in common; a master plan for the upgrading of our science facilities; the adoption of a new policy on scholarly expectations; the establishment of new procedures for faculty hiring; the enhancement of sponsored research; the creation of a mentoring program for all new faculty members; the publication of our first faculty handbook with a variety of new policies, such as those surrounding tenure, promotion, and dismissal; the increase in doctoral graduates to move Baylor into the Doctoral I classification; the establishment of university and distinguished professors; the initiation of a post-doctoral fellows program; the creation of several new centers and institutes, such as the Institute for Studies of Religion; the creation of the Honors College and the Great Texts Program; the increase in the size of the faculty from 580 in 1991 to approximately 750; and, finally, an overall compensation package for faculty members that places Baylor in the top half of the Big XII. I then recognized by name some of the many who helped make these accomplishments possible.

I also sought to explain in my own words to the faculty what I thought my greatest challenge was as chief academic officer: to build a faculty who would gladly embrace the idea of a Christian university and yet at the same time remain outstanding scholars and teachers. This is a particularly difficult undertaking given the nature of advanced graduate training today in the secular research universities from which most of us came. It takes time, I pointed out, for each of us to figure out how it is that we are to love God with our minds as well as our hearts. In addition, we at Baylor are not all of one view on these matters, I said. Many believe that the current administration, myself included as provost, is pressing the religious identity of Baylor too hard, and that as a consequence our academic reputation is being weakened, particularly in regard to faculty issues. Here I turned to Alasdair MacIntyre's *Three Rival Versions of Moral Inquiry* (1990) for guidance. Such debate, he said, is good for us. The university is precisely the place for argument and rigorous conversation—as long as such is done with charity and patience. MacIntyre also affirms that it is moral and theological inquiry that should be central to the university and not relegated to the realm of private belief. So, to those who are anxious about Baylor's direction, I counseled, "Fear not." We are striving to be a university in the largest sense of the word.

I then spoke directly to three cautionary matters that I posed as "dangers." I cautioned, "If Baylor ever loses its mission as a Christian university, we will never regain it." This is a lesson learned from history, but it was given concrete form for me and others from Baylor who had gathered at Harvard and heard the lament of Peter Gomes, whose two *alma maters*, Bates College and Harvard, have both "erased from their souls the very faith that birthed them." Secondly, I cautioned, "As important as disciplines are, they should never be more important than the university itself." I reminded the faculty of the wisdom of John Henry Newman, who, in *The Idea of the University*, wrote about the university being a place of universal knowledge and, though possessing different parts, is in essence one unified body. And, finally, I cautioned, "Within the academic trinity of teaching, research, and service, our increased emphasis at Baylor on research . . . should not be achieved at the price of service, by which I mean primarily the mentoring of students outside of the classroom." This diminution of service and the mentoring of students is often the case in research universities, but, I held, our Christian identity is dependent on the vital interaction of faculty and students. Thus, I said, "there are no short-cuts—we must teach, research, *and* serve."

In the final part of my address I spoke to my own role as provost. "I have taken stock—done an inventory—of my work at Baylor, and have reached the determination that this academic year will be my final year as provost. Therefore, I am announcing today that I will retire from this position at the conclusion of my twelfth year on May 31, 2003." I could not get through this last sentence without becoming emotional. In fact, my emotions were so overwhelming that I had to pause several seconds to get through it. Because I knew this could happen—I have the emotional genes of my father—I came prepared with a safety pin to prick myself at the right moment. It didn't help.

After expressing my apologies to the audience of over 500 faculty and administrators, I proceeded to acknowledge Robert Sloan and his support of my work as provost. I said, "no one has been more important than President Sloan in enabling what has been accomplished here. His leadership has been absolutely essential, and I want to state publically my genuine appreciation for his support." I also noted that I hoped to take on a new task in the years ahead, that of planning and directing a national leadership program for Christian colleges and universities.

I concluded with a word of appreciation to everyone for their "willingness to work with me in common cause," and my final statement, "Thank you, and God bless Baylor!" was followed immediately by a standing ovation.

## REFLECTIONS

I picked up cues by late 2001—more than a year before I announced my retirement—that President Sloan wanted David Jeffrey to be my successor. One factor, of course, was the naming of David as senior vice provost in May of that year. Though I recall this being President Sloan's idea, I certainly supported it. In any case, as a result of David's appointment to our office, we had two great years in the area of faculty recruitment from 2001 to 2003.

Another cue was Sloan's encouraging me to put David in charge of the establishment of the Great Texts program. That puzzled me and I resisted, given that I knew a lot about such programs myself, having worked at the National Endowment for the Humanities for two years, and that I had already asked Scott Moore to coordinate the effort and had asked David to serve on Scott's planning committee. I was perplexed: Why is he asking me to surrender my role as chief academic officer in this case? I refused without ever discussing it with Sloan.

The biggest cue, however, was the appearance of a lengthy article in the November 18, 2002, edition of *Christianity Today*, by the widely known scholar of evangelical Christianity, Randall Balmer, who was then professor of religious history at Columbia University. David had alerted me that such an article might be appearing, but I was not at all prepared for what was published under the title "2012: A School Odyssey: Baylor Strives to Go Where No Christian University Has Gone Before—in Ten Years." Unbeknownst to me, Balmer had spent some time on campus interviewing President Sloan, David, and others, but not me. The article, with a large picture of Sloan and Jeffrey standing together, came across—at least to me—as a kind of celebration of not only the Sloan presidency, but as a coronation of David as the next provost. My name was never mentioned in the entire article.

On the afternoon of the day that I saw the article for the first time, I happened to have arranged a golf outing with Steve Evans. When I told Steve about the article and the fact that my name wasn't even mentioned, he immediately responded: "That's an injustice." Steve said he would write a letter to the editor of *Christianity Today* and call attention to Balmer's oversight, and he did. Steve was joined in the signing of the letter by both David and Mike Beaty. The letter appeared in the next issue of *Christianity Today* under the heading, "Credit at Baylor," which was helpful, but the truth is that the oversight should never have happened in the first place.

# 17

# STANDARDS FOR TENURE

---

The standards for faculty tenure at Baylor had for years been driven primarily by two criteria: excellence in teaching and the demonstration of genuine collegiality. If one performed well in both these areas, and served the requisite number of years, then it was highly probable that one would be granted tenure after the equivalent of six years. Excellence in teaching was judged to a large degree by campus reputation and by student evaluations and, occasionally, by classroom visits from peers. Collegiality was assessed through the day-to-day interactions of non-tenured faculty with tenured faculty members, students, and others in the Baylor community, including one's church. I recall President Reynolds telling me early on that most faculty members at Baylor receive tenure if they get along well with their colleagues. Research and publications could be helpful for gaining tenure, of course, but they were not necessary. Collegiality was.

During the academic year 1996-97, I appointed a task force to engage in a review of our tenure policy to determine if changes needed to be made. The chair of the task force was Greg Benesh, then associate professor of physics, who was also the chair of the university tenure committee at the time. The task force completed its work in May 1997, and upon review of its report by the deans, me, and others in the administration, including the general counsel's office, President Sloan signed off on the revised policy in November 1997.

Some of the revisions were technical in nature, for example, changing the language of "contract" to "letter of appointment." But there were certain emphases that reflected the changing environment at Baylor. One was the new requirement, mentioned in chapter 9, of scholarship. Although scholarship had been emphasized for some years in our doctoral programs and in certain areas of the Hankamer School of Business, by the fall of 1997 scholarship was being required of all tenure-track faculty members who had come to Baylor since 1991, and would be required for all future tenured or tenure-track hires. The revised policy affirmed what was already standard practice at Baylor. The other emphasis of the revised policy was the direct support of Baylor's mission. The tenure policy now stated that the tenure candidate was to submit "a statement of how the candidate supports the goals and mission of the university," which provided the university tenure committee and the administration some meaningful perspective on the candidate's commitment to the Christian mission of Baylor.

On June 14, 2002, five years after the tenure policy revision, an all-day workshop was held in the Law school for the purpose of reviewing and clarifying again the standards for tenure. About seventy people were in attendance, including all the academic deans, all department chairs, and other academic leaders. Our speaker and consultant was Ellen Jackofsky, whose role as associate provost at Southern Methodist University was to oversee the entire tenure process. For the workshop, she was particularly helpful in her comments about scholarship. After all, SMU was no doubt ahead of us in the arena of scholarship and publications—in fact, by quite a bit.

During the course of the workshop, I offered a simple formula for the overall assessment of teaching, research, and service in the granting of tenure. I had given some thought to this matter, but I had not yet offered any specific guideline to the faculty or department heads. Here is what I suggested: a formula of 40–40–20. That is, teaching should count as 40 percent of the evaluation, research should count as 40 percent, and service should count as 20 percent. I reckoned that historically at Baylor the formula was in the range of 60–10–30. I wasn't sure how my proposed formula would be received, the concern being, I thought, about the 40 percent for research and scholarship. We had an open discussion about the overall formula, at which point Jackofsky offered in total candor that at SMU it would probably be 49–49–2. She wasn't kidding. As she went on to discuss the issue with respect to SMU, it certainly came across that she thought that SMU's lack of consideration regarding service in tenure decisions was a regrettable circumstance.

In my annual address to the faculty at its fall meeting, and written later in the faculty senate newsletter of November 2002, I reflected on this aspect of our June workshop on standards for tenure. I wrote the following:

> The increased importance of research and scholarly/creative activity should not be gained at the expense of service. The service component should perhaps not be weighted as heavily for tenure-track faculty as for tenured faculty, specifically because tenure-track faculty members should not be asked to assume any major committee assignments during the first three years of their appointments. However, the service component for tenure-track faculty members should nevertheless still clearly emphasize the importance, within the context of Baylor's mission, of student mentoring, interpersonal relationships, general university citizenship and support, and service to their professional field, the local community, and a local congregation.

I then offered this observation: "Because the mission of Baylor is intimately connected to our religious identity, a tenure candidate must give evidence of a faithful commitment both to a local congregation and to the mission of Baylor as a Christian university. These two elements are linked because the beliefs and practices of both should be mutually complementary."

A major outcome of the workshop was a call for every department and/or school to develop appropriate criteria and guidelines in the area of scholarship for tenure-track faculty members. These criteria and guidelines were to be recommended to the appropriate dean by December 2, 2002, and reflect the fact that standards for tenure at Baylor—in teaching, research, and service—were higher than ever before. The main task now, I observed, was to clarify, with appropriate consistency across all the departments and schools, the expectations of faculty members who hold tenure-track appointments.

## REFLECTIONS

Alongside my article about standards for tenure, the Faculty Senate Newsletter included a response from the chair of the Faculty Senate, Charles Weaver. Chuck expressed words of appreciation for my willingness to comment on our standards for tenure, as well as my directive to all departments to develop criteria by which the faculty of the various academic units would be assessed. This was a "positive step," he said, and he encouraged the faculty "to take the central role in this process."

Then he continued, "One area that remains elusive—and not coincidentally generates tremendous anxiety among tenure-track faculty—is the degree to which one 'contributes to the mission of the university.'" While publications are quantifiable and teaching effectiveness is somewhat public and hence objective, mission-related activity is much less so and thereby can present problems in its assessment. Chuck concluded with this observation: "I have always been more comfortable evaluating a colleague's *behavior* than his or her sincerity of faith."

The reason that I call attention to this exchange is to stress the importance of good relations with the leadership of the faculty, by which I mean primarily but not exclusively the Faculty Senate. For example, I co-authored an article, "Tenure Development Plan," with Jay Losey, another chair of the Faculty Senate, that was published in the November 2000 senate newsletter. In addition, I met with the chair and vice chair of the Faculty Senate once a month to review issues and concerns that we were facing as a university. Perhaps the most important interaction was my policy, instituted in 1991-92, that the chair of the faculty senate be a regular member of the Council of Deans. The council met once a month and the chair of the senate was always given a place on the agenda of our meetings.

When I stepped down as provost at the end of May 2003, I was flowered with numerous accolades and given plaques, but none meant more to me than the recognition I received on March 18, 2003, in a meeting of the Faculty Senate. Chuck Weaver presented a beautiful plaque inscribed with the words "in recognition of twelve years of distinguished service as Provost of Baylor University and with appreciation for his commitment to academic integrity." These words were followed with the names and signatures of the twelve chairs of the Faculty Senate with whom I worked for one year each, beginning in 1991-92 and concluding in 2002-03: Terry S. Maness, Dianna M. Vitanza, Douglas W. Rogers, Raymond J. Cannon, Kathy R. Hillman, E. Jeter Basden, J. Christopher Buddo, Daniel B. McGee, Robert M. Baird, Jay B. Losey, David L. Longfellow, and Charles A. Weaver III. I was particularly moved that all of these former chairs were present at the meeting. Needless to say, it was another emotional moment.

# 18

# A COLLOQUY ON THE BAPTIST AND CHRISTIAN CHARACTER OF BAYLOR

———————

At the Council of Deans' meeting of October 2, 2002, in the fall after I announced my retirement, I distributed copies of articles presented at Notre Dame, in 1994, which focused on the Catholic character of the institution and its relationship to such issues as faculty hiring and tenure. Using the Notre Dame "conversation" model, I suggested that the Council of Deans devote its entire November agenda to a similar discussion regarding the character of Baylor as a Baptist/Christian university and to consider applications useful to Baylor, particularly regarding what we were looking for in new faculty and tenured faculty.

I began the November meeting of the Council of Deans with a prepared statement in which I summarized papers by Ralph McInerny and Thomas Flint, both professors of philosophy at Notre Dame. Here is what I said:

> Ralph McInerny argues that it is virtually impossible today to be a university without being Catholic. This is the case, he holds, because "every activity we engage in is subject to both technical and moral appraisal." By "technical appraisal" he means the judgments

we make in the university about and within our specific disciplines, about the methodologies and the subject matters in which the technical disciplines are grounded. By "moral appraisal" he means the broader criteria which characterize our common university life, the moral ambience which provides the setting for and gives purpose to our work taken as a whole. That we trust each other, for example, suggests the centrality of the moral foundation of the university. For McInerny, these two categories of activity of the university—technical appraisal and moral appraisal—rest on two presuppositions within the Catholic university: (1) that there is such a thing as truth and that we should seek it; and (2) that there is such a thing as moral truth which is accessible to all.

The problem, however, is that the modern university is beset with moral relativism and epistemological nihilism. Moral judgments, it is widely believed in the academy and in the wider culture, have no objective standing (just personal preferences). Knowledge and the search for truth are ultimately vacuous activities, human constructions having no appeal beyond themselves. (This is particularly evident in disciplines focusing on "theory," such as literary theory, social theory, political theory, philosophy of science, and the like.) In sum, McInerny asserts "there are two things which are fundamentally destructive of what a university is, the denial of common morality and the denial of objective truth." The Christian beliefs in God and in the reality of the moral community strike an entirely different view on both counts.

McInerny concludes: "There are dangers to the university today, but they do not arise from religious belief. Moral relativism and epistemological nihilism are destructive of the university at its very roots. In countering these, in having the heart to confront them, not simply to anathematize them, the university has its greatest ally in the Catholic faith. The best thing that ever happened to the human mind is the Catholic faith." And that is because "the best thing that ever happened to the human race is the saving act of Jesus Christ."

This summary of McInerny's position provides an important background for Thomas Flint's principle of "Significant Contribution." As outlined by G. M. Hamburg, Significant Contribution may be summarized as follows: For purposes of faculty evaluation (hiring, reappointment, tenure, promotion), faculty members should demonstrate that they will make or are making a Significant Contribution to the Catholic character of Notre Dame. So-called "generic questions" would typically be asked at critical points in the evaluation of faculty: How are the faculty member's research projects influenced by his or her Christian belief? Are the topics of investigation ones of special interest to Christians? How does one's faith relate to the enterprise of teaching? Will the teaching one does contribute in some special way to our students' growth as Catholic intellectuals?

According to Flint, Significant Contribution is not to be understood as either a necessary or a sufficient condition for hiring, renewal, tenure, or promotion. Significant Contribution is but one of many factors to be considered in faculty evaluation. However, to ignore a faculty member's contribution to the Catholic character of Notre Dame "makes no more sense than to ignore his or her record as a teacher or researcher."

When I finished with this statement, I turned to each of the deans and to the chair of the Faculty Senate for questions and issues they wished to discuss. Each one spoke, reflecting on the Notre Dame conversation and on his or her own experience at Baylor.

I do not recall the specifics of the discussion that ensued, but I do recall the outcome: The Council of Deans wanted to continue the conversation but enlarge it to include, somehow, the entire faculty of the university. The approach that immediately drew strong support was the idea of a conference of the kind held at Notre Dame in 1994. The title for the conference seemed obvious: "A Colloquy on the Baptist and Christian Character of Baylor." This event would be sponsored by the Council of Deans, under the leadership of the Law school and its dean, Brad Toben.

It is important to keep in mind the larger context for the discussion at the Council of Deans' meeting in November 2002: *Baylor 2012* (see chapter 14). Though *Baylor 2012* was approved unanimously by the Board of Regents on September 21, 2001, the response of the faculty was not one of unanimous support. Of course, I was aware of some of the objections at the time, but after a year of implementation, the resistance to *Baylor 2012* seemed to become more and more pronounced. Here is how Dean Toben would put it in his foreword to *The Baptist and Christian Character of Baylor* (2003), a published volume of essays from the conference itself:

> A deep divide of opinion and sentiment congealed quickly around Baylor 2012. The ensuing discussion has found its content in good-faith expressions of deeply held conviction as well as in sometimes biting statements, both public and private, either supporting or taking aim at the vision. The discussion or—for an institution that prides itself on being the "Baylor family"—perhaps

more appropriately, the argument continues to unfold in all manner of venues.

Because of this disunity, there was certainly strong motivation to revisit again the essential mission of our university, in particular the continuing relevance of our religious identity. In addition, because the conference, held on April 10–11, 2003, corresponded to my stepping down as provost, the Council of Deans decided to subtitle the event "A Colloquy in Honor of Dr. Donald D. Schmeltekopf, Provost & Vice President for Academic Affairs, Baylor University, 1991–2003." Indeed, it was a great honor

I was directly involved in the planning of the colloquy along with Brad Toben, Larry Lyon, and others. The opening session, "A University in the Largest Sense of the Word," was borrowed from John Henry Newman's classic work, *The Idea of the University*, in which he argued that the subject matter of the true university is God, Nature, and Man—though, of course, for the program we used the term "human beings." The typical modern university is not a university in the largest sense of the word because it tends to bracket out the pursuit of moral and religious truth as part of its responsibility. The Christian university—for example, Baylor—can do no such thing. Moreover, we at a Christian university should always be looking for connections between disciplines and sub-disciplines in pursuit of inter-disciplinary approaches and integrative perspectives. While specializations are important, we should avoid "knowledge standing by itself." As Newman pointed out, all knowledge finds its ultimate unity in God. If God is taken out of the equation, we get mere specialization and hence fragmentation and intellectual incoherence. Furthermore, "there is no community of scholars, and the realm of values is reduced to personal preference."

Stephen Evans was recruited to offer the position paper for the opening session and his paper reflected precisely these concerns about the modern university and the need for the "connectedness of knowledge." Here he stressed the importance of theology. If theology is removed from the university, the whole structure of knowledge is incomplete and thereby harmed. But, Evans held, this is a contested idea in the contemporary university setting. Therefore, we must understand that the context for the Christian university today is one of a diversity of institutions, a competition, so to speak, of varied "narratives." Within this context, the Christian university, and "the grand Christian story" which undergirds it, is particularly important given the contours of American higher education in our time.

The purpose of the second session of the colloquy, "Baylor as a Baptist and Christian University: Faculty Hiring, Tenure and Promotion," was to ask, if it is true that a Christian university is a university in the largest sense of the word, what sort of faculty members are best suited to flourish in such an academic community? We recruited two speakers for this session, Mikeal Parsons, professor of religion, and Robert Baird, professor and chair of philosophy. Parsons noted that there are distinctions to be made between "Baptist" and "Christian" when applied to a university. The word "Baptist" suggests matters of religious style, such as freedom of conscience and non-creedalism. The word "Christian" points to matters of religious substance, common to all Christian denominations, such as belief in the One Triune God and the efficacy of Christ's death and resurrection for sinful human beings. At Baylor, Parsons noted, these two are often applied together and in some tension. His main emphasis, however, was to comment on the notion of the "Significant Contribution Model" elaborated by Thomas Flint at the Notre Dame conference of 1994. Parsons argued that faculty members at Baylor should be hired and evaluated, at least in part, based on an assessment of their contribution to the Baptist and Christian character of Baylor.

In contrast to Parsons, Baird advocated a more fluid set of boundaries than those currently in place at Baylor. He held that we at Baylor should recognize the intellectual benefits of hiring and granting tenure to faculty members who may not be "vigorous in the life of faith" or who may be of non-Christian religions or of no religion at all. Baird gave examples of distinguished professors, such as Charles Hartshorne, metaphysician and philosopher of religion, and Michael Ruse, philosopher of science, who, given their own religious perspectives, would likely not be hired at Baylor today because of what Baird labelled "this intense emphasis on the religious criterion." While acknowledging the potential risks such hires might bring our university, Baird concluded by advocating "a more open hiring policy."

For the third session, "What Does It Mean to Support Baylor's Mission?" Owen Lind, professor of biology, and Ralph Wood, university professor of theology and literature, each offered position papers. Lind focused on the impact of research on our institutional mission primarily in relation to the distinctive presidencies of Abner McCall (1961–1981), Herbert Reynolds (1981–1995), and Robert Sloan (1995–present). During the McCall years, Lind reported, research was essentially neglected at Baylor. During the Reynolds era, research was encouraged. But during the Sloan years, at least up to the time of the colloquy, research was required.

Lind applauded the Sloan years, excited that finally his own calling as a research scientist was, under *Baylor 2012*, clearly integral to Baylor's mission. He cautioned, however, that given the anti-religious bias in most scientific fields, religious qualifications for faculty hiring in the sciences may need to be somewhat relaxed.

Wood's paper addressed the issue of Baylor's Christian mission in relation to the obligations of faculty and administrators to support that mission, particularly with regard to church involvement. Wood contended that there is nothing to fear in the university's requirement that faculty members and administrators alike be practicing members of a local church. Rightly understood, the church is the universal Body of Christ in which, he said, we find "Truth large enough to ground and inspire and direct our entire academic life, and Community large enough to include everyone except those who refuse to enter it." This notion of the "church catholic" finds its expression in the "church specific," the local congregation. In the local church we plumb the depths of human understanding far beyond that of our academic disciplines. Wood went on to argue that the university, under the leadership of administrators, especially senior ones, must seek to serve "the Kingdom of God in its largest ecumenical reach, not in any parochial sense." While maintaining our strengths as Baptists, we must, he said, become "an ever-more ecumenically Christian university."

A grand reception and dinner were held in the elegant Barfield Drawing Room of the Bill Daniel Student Center following the second session. The invited speaker for this occasion was David Solomon, the H. B. and W. P. White Director of the Center for Ethics and Culture at the University of Notre Dame, and former visiting distinguished professor at Baylor. I personally recruited David for this assignment because of his enormous help to me in making the deep connections with Notre Dame that are evident throughout these pages. Of course, the planning group for the colloquy supported my desire to invite David's participation in the colloquy.

David Solomon is a Baylor graduate, class of 1964. After his PhD studies at the University of Texas, he was immediately recruited to the philosophy department at Notre Dame, where he has spent his entire academic career. After reviewing some of this personal background in his talk, David said the following:

> We are here to do two things—first, to celebrate the career of Don Schmeltekopf, and second, to do it by having a knock-down drag out argument [about Christian higher education]. This is a curious

tradition in academic life to honor a beloved colleague by arguing over his bones—not that Don has been reduced to mere bones yet. Let me begin by saying a few things about Don, and then I will ease into the argument.

And say a few things about me he did. What he said was high praise and actually quite humbling. I'll give one example and then move on to his formal remarks which he called "The Renewal of Christian Higher Education." Solomon described a conference held at Notre Dame the previous year in which a panel of three university presidents, Robert Sloan, Father Edward Malloy (of Notre Dame), and Charles Dougherty (of Duquesne), spoke about the future of Christian higher education in the United States. He related how surprised those in attendance were, especially a number of Baylor students, that it was not Notre Dame or Duquesne that generated the most discussion, but Baylor. Then Solomon remarked, "Don Schmeltekopf has changed the perception of Baylor in the world of higher education." Perhaps some would disagree with him, but it was a great compliment.

David gave the remainder of his talk to a critique of the major papers of the colloquy, but he gave special attention to the one by Bob Baird. First, to say that Baylor's religious identity is secure, as Baird argued, is "naïve," according to Solomon. Whether or not Baylor is able to climb within the ranks of research universities, the fact remains that faculty hiring, in terms of sustaining a genuine Christian identity, is extremely difficult in today's academic environment. Persistence in hiring faculty who fit Baylor's mission will simply be necessary for the foreseeable future. Second, on Solomon's reading, Baird believes Notre Dame's hiring is "much more permissive than Baylor's and that Notre Dame nevertheless achieved academic excellence without oversight. If loose oversight is good enough for the Notre Dame goose, why not for the Baylor gander?" Solomon's response was to say that faculty hiring at Notre Dame is "in trouble." The reigning criterion is now "elevated standards." Standards are killing us, he said, because that criterion trumps all others, including Notre Dame's Catholic character. The Baird vision might well remain the goal, but, "unfortunately," Solomon claimed, "I feel that in order to build a university that embraces both the highest intellectual standards and the deepest Christian commitment, we now have to be more intentional in its design."

The various papers and responses of the colloquy were collected in the volume, *The Baptist and Christian Character of Baylor*, coedited by my colleague, Dianna Vitanza, and me, along with Brad Toben who wrote the foreword. I also wrote the introductory chapter, "A Christian University in the Baptist Tradition: History of a Vision," and concluded my essay with the following lines:

> The good news for Baylor is that we are being intentional about our future as a preeminent Baptist and Christian university. The colloquy of April 10–11, 2003, was a grand and successful conversation about a contested idea, the meaning of a Christian university and its role in the landscape of American higher education.

It was indeed a grand and successful conversation. And what was especially satisfying to me was that, as Dianna and I said in our preface, "the intellectual weight of the colloquy was provided overwhelmingly by Baylor faculty members who represent diverse perspectives on the issues."

# 19

# EXIT

---

The final few weeks of my tenure as provost were filled with special events and speaking opportunities. I was recognized in several contexts for my service as provost, as was to be expected, but one event stands out as particularly meaningful—a reception in my honor on May 8, 2003, in the Barfield Drawing Room. A large crowd had gathered, but I was especially pleased that many of my own family members were there, including my children and their spouses, my grandchildren, my brothers and sisters-in-law, and my sister from North Carolina. President Sloan made remarks, as did Paulette Edwards who gave me a large book of letters from faculty and staff, and then Sloan presented a huge silver tray to me commemorating my years as provost. Engraved on the tray are the words, "To Donald D. Schmeltekopf, Provost & Vice President for Academic Affairs, In Appreciation of your significant and lasting contributions to Baylor University, 1990–2003, The Baylor University Family, May 8, 2003." It was yet another deeply moving moment.

For the last executive council retreat I attended, held on March 4–5, 2003, President Sloan asked me to offer the opening devotional. I entitled my reflection, "Creating an Alternative to Vice Presidential Power Politics." Having been in vice presidential-level positions for seventeen years, I had come to some conclusions about the virtues needed and fitting for vice presidents, virtues grounded in our communal life as Christians. By "vice presidential power politics," I meant "the complex of relationships and the varieties of conduct carried out by vice presidents in their common quest for power and influence within the institutions they serve." I noted that politics of this sort applies to President Bush's cabinet, to the headquarters of IBM, to the Baptist General Convention of Texas office in Dallas, and to this executive council. An important factor underlying this "common quest for power and influence" are certain personality characteristics all vice presidents I have known share: they are without exception strong-willed, competitive, and purpose-driven people. On the other hand, I said, I have yet to know one who is a milquetoast.

I called these features "personality characteristics," and as such, I claimed, they are by and large morally neutral. The issue "is how people of such a personality live out these characteristics as vice presidents." I then laid out two approaches that can serve as the background to vice presidential relations. One I labelled the view of self-interested reason alone. Here I quoted from Machiavelli's *The Prince*, where he advocated the notion of cleverness as an essential virtue of the leader. I gave as an example my own experience at the New Jersey Board of Higher Education in the early 1980s. The vice presidential-level officers were, or seemed to be, in a state of war, albeit disguised, with one another. This was not seen as a problem by the chancellor, who allowed the conflicts to play out and then made the decisions himself.

I drew three "lessons" from this dark side of vice presidential politics. The first is the use of fear to gain advantage which follows Machiavelli's dictum that "it is better to be feared than loved." The second lesson is to disguise one's motives in pursuit of self-interest. The Prince, Machiavelli said, should not keep his word when keeping it is to his disadvantage. The third lesson is to practice duplicity. Machiavelli believed that it is all-important for rulers to appear to be a certain kind of ruler (or vice president), to seem to be merciful, loyal, humane, upright, and even religious rather than actually practice those qualities. The worst sort of Prince is one who has integrity.

Probably the most widespread idea used in secular management theory today for dealing with this dark side of vice presidential politics is to liken vice presidents collectively to a "team." This team concept, I contended, is supposed to help us overcome the vices that accompany the blatant self-interest often operating in vice presidential politics. And to an extent, the team metaphor is helpful: we clearly must work together cooperatively in the pursuit of common goals. But the team concept has at least two serious limitations, both of which are disguised forms of self-interest. Teams don't have presidents as one of their players. The role of president is not analogous to that of coach, since the president is most definitely one of the participants, indeed the most important one, rather than an observer or encourager. So, the team concept collapses on itself. The second limitation relates to the structure of accountability for vice presidents and presidents that is not fully analogous to the team concept. In sports, teams win or lose; but with vice presidents and presidents, some of us can win, so to speak, and some of us can lose, so to speak, because of the offices we hold and the accountability attached to those offices.

What we need, I argued, is an alternative to the concept of the team in vice presidential relations, namely, the sense of Christian community. Here I drew on Eph 4:1–7 and 11–16. The model that Paul offers was not that of the corporate team but of the confessing church. As such, it entails not only individual virtues but communal qualities. What are these shared communal qualities? First, we share a confessing common faith—we are brothers and sisters united in Christ, each with our own calling and work, but we all share the same faith. Second, we are all forgiven sinners, and hence we share the need for humility. We should always pursue our work "with all lowliness and meekness, with patience, forbearing one another in love," as Paul tells us. Third, we vice presidents should listen to one another when we speak and when we are not speaking. This close and deep listening can be a source of great wisdom. And, fourth, we should pray for one another. When we pray for one another—by name—we are submitting our wills, ambition, cunning, and whatever we vice presidents carry with us every day, to God for his transformation and use. Genuine prayer has the power to convert us so that we can indeed "be joined and knit together in love."

I closed my devotional with these words: "So, there is indeed a clear alternative to self-interested vice presidential politics and today I am grateful that I have had the opportunity to work with all of you within a living Christian community and share together its qualities and virtues." We then prayed as each was led to do so, and we all were, beginning with President Sloan.

My final day in office was May 31, 2003. I was succeeded as provost by David Jeffrey, senior vice provost and distinguished professor of literature and humanities. My transition to a new role—Provost Emeritus and also the Hazel and Harry Chavanne Professor of Christian Ethics in

Business—went smoothly. I had been granted a sabbatical through December 2003, with the commitment to teach business ethics in the management department in the Hankamer School of Business beginning January 2004. My sabbatical officially commenced with a six-week stay at Christ College in Oxford and time in Rome. I had visited Oxford eight consecutive years, beginning in 1994, for a combination of vacation and reading/study. In fact, one regular activity for me during my previous summer visits to Oxford was the preparation of my speeches for the fall faculty meetings. Judy was always my first audience.

# EPILOGUE ONE

Judy and I departed for London on July 7, 2003. Little did we know that we were getting out of town at an opportune time. A huge controversy had erupted in the Baylor athletic department—specifically, the men's basketball program—when one player on the team, Carlton Dotson, shot and killed another player, his roommate, Patrick Dennehy. The killing occurred near an old gravel pit where the two young men were engaged in pistol shooting. This killing, in fact, a murder, occurred in mid-June and became a national headline. A *New York Times* article of August 28 summarized the matter in the following fashion:

> When a basketball player at the world's largest Baptist university was shot twice in the head near an old gravel pit and his former teammate was arrested and charged with pulling the trigger, the event seemed dramatic enough to open a beach holiday page turner. And then the story unfolded, layer by layer, to expose the lying coach, the cheating program, drugs, secret tapes, clandestine meetings and an attempted cover-up at Baylor University.

The article goes on to quote President Sloan: "We ask ourselves, How did it happen?" The *Times* story notes that this question came from "the embattled Baylor president" in a conference room outside his office "as some faculty members publicly called for his resignation."

The "embattled" president would face more attacks in an event called "The Baylor Family Dialogue," held on July 18, 2003, in Baylor's Farrell Center, the venue for both basketball games and our commencements. The event was organized by the Baylor Alumni Association, featuring a wide array of speakers as panelists, including Drayton McLane, who was then chair of the Board of Regents, Robert Sloan, David Jeffrey, and David Brooks, vice president for finance, all representing the administration. Representing alumni were Bette McCall Miller, daughter of former Baylor president Abner McCall; Jim Patton, chair and professor of psychology/neuroscience; Kent Reynolds, son of former Baylor president Herbert Reynolds; and Glenn Biggs, businessman and former chair of the regents. According to the *Baylor Magazine* story of the event, Bette McCall Miller charged that President Sloan's "move toward creedalism is a page taken from the fundamentalist's handbook." David Jeffrey "rebuked" these charges, calling them slanderous.

Jim Patton urged, again according to the *Baylor Magazine*, more "finesse" in the interview process for new faculty members, especially regarding religious matters, suggesting that the interview process be conducted "in a more courteous fashion." Perhaps the most overt criticism of the administration came from Glenn Biggs, who contended that there were "serious flaws in the administration." Then Biggs said, "At some point, you have to grade the leadership. This administration has not been able to keep the focus and bring all the people together." But that was not the view of Drayton McLane, who stated that early on in the Sloan presidency the board encouraged the president to develop a strategic plan for Baylor's future, to "boldly put a stake in the ground and proclaim what Baylor University is." That's what *Baylor 2012* did.

So, while I was in Oxford enjoying the delights of a summer in England, it seemed that a growing wave of opposition to the administration began to catalyze, emotionally and tactically, around the basketball scandal and some of the rhetoric of the so-called "Baylor Family Dialogue." In the background of the latter, however, was the vexing issue of how an institution deals with major change without some people feeling and/or being marginalized. The Baylor of 2003 was not the same as the Baylor of 1990. *Baylor 2012* was the explicit manifestation of this fact, and a lot of folks in the Baylor community didn't like the changes nor the direction Baylor was heading. That included many alumni, many retired faculty members and administrators, many tenured faculty members, and apparently many others.

Elsewhere I have described the divide as being between "traditionalists," those who embraced Baylor's longstanding institutional identity as primarily an undergraduate university with strong professional programs, and "progressives," those who embraced and continue to embrace what can be called simply a serious research university, but with the all-important modifier, *Christian*, that is, a Christian research university. This divide in our institutional self-understanding persisted for the next several years, creating the conditions for institutional instability. This was aggravated by instability in the administration, at least from 2004 until about 2010. Today, in 2015, thankfully, Baylor seems to be on the other side of institutional instability—indeed, Baylor's impressive academic and athletic achievements continue to make national headlines—but the question of our religious identity will always be fraught with an element of uncertainty. On this front, we can never assume there will be no threats. *We must always be faithful to our Christian mission.*

# EPILOGUE TWO

I n the spring of 2005, David Jeffrey, then provost, spoke to me about taking over the directorship of the Center for Ministry Effectiveness upon the retirement of Winfred Moore. Our conversation, however, broadened to include a larger initiative I wanted to pursue. In my faculty address announcing my retirement, I had indicated my desire to develop a national leadership program for Christian colleges and universities. President Sloan and I had discussed this idea on several occasions, and now in my discussions with David, we determined jointly that the work of the center would be expanded to include this broader vision for Christian higher education. The center's name would reflect this change as well; we called it the "Center for Ministry Effectiveness and Educational Leadership." I assumed the directorship of the center on June 1, 2006.

During my years in higher education I had been a participant in several major leadership programs. Prior to my Baylor career, I was a fellow in the American Council on Education (ACE) program on academic leadership during the year 1982–1983. Then, after arriving in Waco, President Reynolds had encouraged me to participate in a variety of leadership development programs, which included one at Texas A & M, one in Colorado Springs, Colorado, and one at Harvard University. All of these, including especially the ACE program, were enormously beneficial to me in gaining a broad understanding of the major issues and challenges in higher education, particularly in the role of an administrator. In addition, these programs included elements of self-knowledge (even, in one, an IQ test) and approaches to understanding the qualities of strong and effective leaders.

Along with these experiences, and together with about twenty years of academic administration, I was deeply influenced by the writings of Mark Schwehn, George Marsden, James Burtchaell, and others on the plight of Christian higher education in America as it existed in the 1980s and 1990s. Schwehn argued in *Exiles from Eden: Religion and the Academic Vocation in America* (1993) that by stressing research—the making and transmitting of knowledge—American higher education had abandoned its traditional mission of shaping moral character. Marsden showed in *The Soul of the American University* (1994) how the demise of the dominant Christian culture over the last two centuries had prompted many Christian colleges and universities—from Harvard to Wake Forest—to jettison their religious identity and secularize. Burtchaell's *The Dying of the Light* (1998) affirmed the essential features of Marsden's narrative, showing in numerous case studies how educational enterprises sponsored by Christian denominations shed their denominational affiliations over time, including Baptist initiatives. These works confirmed what I was seeing with my own eyes and, to some extent, experiencing personally during my time as provost.

Another all-important factor influencing my commitment to the future of Christian higher education was my active involvement for many years in the International Association of Baptist Colleges and Universities (IABCU), which made it possible for me to get to know many presidents, provosts, deans, and others in Baptist higher education. Within this network, I began in 2006 to discuss the possibility of organizing a leadership program specifically for Baptist colleges/universities, first in Texas and then throughout the country. My initial discussions were limited to the provosts of the Texas Baptist schools, eight in number, with the help and endorsement of the Baptist General Convention of Texas. We decided to call the program the "Seminar on Academic Leadership in Baptist Universities."

The program was a success from the start. Our first seminar in May 2007 was a five-day program hosted by Mary Hardin-Baylor University. Twenty-five participants from the various Texas Baptist universities gathered on the Mary Hardin-Baylor campus for a stimulating week of lectures, discussion, case studies, and vigorous interaction. After the first year, the seminar was always held in Waco at Baylor with basically the same format. Funding for the seminar came from participants' enrollment fees (250 dollars the first year, 500 dollars later), as well as funding from outside entities, including the Baptist General Convention of Texas, the International Association of Baptist Colleges and Universities, and the Lilly Fellows Program for the Arts and Humanities at Valparaiso University. Baylor was also generous in its support of the seminar, giving us complete access to academic buildings and student living accommodations without charge.

As director of the seminar, I always opened the program with a brief talk I called "Leadership in Baptist Colleges and Universities," offering a historical background of the founding of the Baptist colleges and universities in the United States, the earliest of which was Rhode Island College (now Brown University). I pointed out every year the fact that Baptist colleges and universities in the South maintained their Baptist connections much more so than in the North and Midwest. This explained, I held, why Baptist universities in the South are still by and large connected to the church, while the same is not the case elsewhere. Nevertheless, I noted, several of our southern Baptist schools have cut their denominational ties, including Richmond, Wake Forest, Stetson, Furman, and Meredith. And then I said that the underlying purpose of the seminar is to help stop this trend in Baptist life, indeed, elsewhere as well.

The final seminar I directed, always with the able assistance of Julie Covington, was in May 2014. The average attendance at each seminar was slightly over thirty participants, yielding a grand total of 250 over seven years. The participants came from across the United States, and even foreign countries, but overwhelmingly they came from the southern states and California. The program was filled with outstanding speakers, including Robert Benne (Roanoke College), Bill Brian (Texas A&M), Susan Felch (Calvin College), Susan VanZanten (Seattle Pacific), Paul Corts (Council of Christian Colleges and Universities), Mark Schwehn (Valparaiso), and Darryl Tippens (Pepperdine). Several Baylor faculty and administrators were also a regular part of our program, including Charles Beckenhauer (general counsel), Elizabeth Davis (provost, now president of Furman), Robyn Driskell (associate dean), and Robert Kruschwitz (philosophy professor). The underlying theme throughout the seminar was the absolute importance of upholding the Christian mission of our schools.

Did the seminar help produce leaders for our Baptist schools? The answer is yes, without question. Today the overwhelming majority of the program's alumni serve as Baptist university presidents, provosts, deans, department chairs, and the like. Some of the participants, of course, came to the seminar already holding administrative positions, but a large number have assumed higher levels of responsibility since participating in the program. This was made concretely evident at the annual meeting of the

IABCU in June 2014, in Charleston, South Carolina, when those in attendance were asked to stand if they had been participants in our leadership
seminar. At least fifty stood up.

The crowning recognition of my work in Christian higher education
occurred at this same meeting on the campus of Charleston Southern University when I was given The Charles D. Johnson Award for Distinguished
Contribution to Baptist-Related Higher Education by the International
Association of Baptist Colleges and Universities. The award came with a
beautiful plaque and a considerable cash gift. The public announcement
about the award included the following:

> Mike Arrington, retiring executive director of the IABCU, praised
> Schmeltekopf for his long and faithful service to Baptist-related
> higher education and to the Association as a former board member
> and as board chair from 1998–1999. Through the annual "Seminar
> on Academic Leadership in Baptist Universities," held on the Bay-
> lor University campus, Schmeltekopf has trained more than 250
> administrators for their work at Baptist colleges and universities.

I was enormously pleased to receive the Charles D. Johnson Award,
which was a surprise, and I was also pleased that Judy and several colleagues from Baylor were there to join in the celebration. Abner McCall is
the only other Baylor person to have received this award in its long history.
*Gloria Deo!*

CPSIA information can be obtained
at www.ICGtesting.com
Printed in the USA
FSHW011945031019
62687FS

9 781498 231763